"Debby hits the nail on the head when she asks us to consider what it means to be wholehearted in our love and devotion to the One who is wholehearted in His love for us. Her clear writing, insightful scriptural teaching, and her obvious wholehearted love for the Father will draw you to pursue Him with your whole heart, nothing held in reserve."

—JENNIFER KENNEDY DEAN,
executive director, the Praying Life Foundation,
author of best-selling Live a Praying Life™

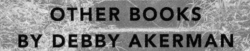

OTHER BOOKS
BY DEBBY AKERMAN

Hold On:
Finding Peace and Reward
When God Has Us Waiting on Him

SECRETS

to

SURRENDER

Living Wholeheartedly

DEBBY AKERMAN

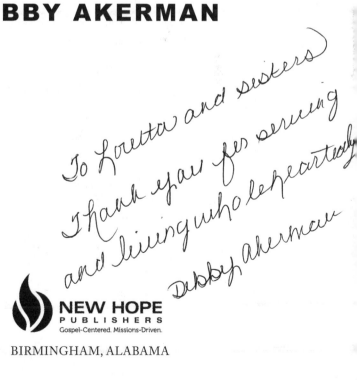

To Loretta and sisters)
Thank you for serving
and living wholeheartedly
Debby Akerman

NEW HOPE
PUBLISHERS
Gospel-Centered. Missions-Driven.

BIRMINGHAM, ALABAMA

New Hope® Publishers
PO Box 12065
Birmingham, AL 35202-2065
NewHopeDigital.com
New Hope Publishers is a division of WMU®.

Library of Congress Control Number: 2013955342

Cover Image: Jon Bilous/shutterstock.com

ISBN-10: 1-59669-406-8
ISBN-13: 978-1-59669-406-4

N144111 • 0414 • 4M1

THIS BOOK IS DEDICATED *to four women whose lives have been lived wholeheartedly for the Lord and who have mentored me for leadership: Susan Brindle, Jacque Kirchoff, Beulah Peoples, and Evelyn Blount. Each of these women has been instrumental in various stages of my life. They have challenged me to serve the Lord wholeheartedly and have affirmed my call to missions.*

TABLE OF CONTENTS

ACKNOWLEDGMENTS

GOD HAS FAITHFULLY KEPT His promise given to me for these years serving Him in 2 Corinthians 9:8 (NIV 1984): "And God is able to make all grace abound to you, so that in all things at all times, having all that you need, you will abound in every good work." *Secrets to Surrender* has indeed been a work that God poured into me through His Holy Word and by His Holy Spirit.

Going deeper with God to live wholeheartedly for Him is seldom a solitary journey. The secrets to surrender are seen in the testimonies of surrendered lives past and present. I am very grateful for the willingness of each who contributed their testimonies to personalize the call of God to us to surrender, sacrifice, and serve. I deeply appreciate WMU and New Hope Publishers for entrusting me with the writing of this book and encouraging me each step of the way. How thankful I am for the love, encouragement, and prayers of my very supportive husband, Brad, who has patiently seen me through the hundreds of hours secluded in my study. And knowing my faithful prayer partners were interceding daily on my behalf enabled me to stay the course of writing this book.

FOREWORD

❦

W E SERVE AN ALL-OR-NOTHING GOD. He gives Himself wholly to us. Not piecemeal. Not as we deserve it. The minute we open our lives to Him, He's all in.

I love that. He is fully present to us every second, no intermissions. Not for the blink of an eye does He turn away. Not one drop of His power and provision is ever, ever unavailable to us. He loves us wholeheartedly and is wholeheartedly devoted to each one of His children as if each one were His only concern.

Paul makes this reasoned argument. "He who did not spare his own Son, but gave him up for us all—how will he not also, along with him, graciously give us all things?" (Romans 8:32). Paul is directly referencing Genesis 22:16, God's words to Abraham after his obedience in offering Isaac: "Because you have done this and have not withheld your son, your only son."

Do you think Abraham owned anything—even his own life— that he would not have given gladly in place of his son, his only son, Isaac, whom he loved? Once Abraham's willingness to give God his only son had been put on display for the ages, was there any question that everything Abraham owned was God's for the asking? Paul draws upon this account, brings it over into the present moment, and says, "He who did not spare his own Son, but gave him up for us all—how will he not also, along with him, graciously give us all things?" (Romans 8:32).

"This is how God showed his love among us: He sent his one and only Son into the world that we might live through him. This is love: not that we loved God, but that he loved us and sent his Son as an atoning sacrifice for our sins" (1 John 4:9–10). Is there anything left for Him to prove?

The Hebrew word used in Genesis 22, translated "withhold," is the word *chasak*. The word means "to hold back for your own personal use" or "to keep in reserve." The word shares a primary Hebrew letter with the word usually translated "holy" (*qadash*), which means "to be completely set apart, to be consecrated for a specific use." Abraham did not set Isaac aside to keep him completely and wholly for himself. He did not keep Isaac in his two-fisted grasp and say, "Mine! All mine!" He didn't consider Isaac "holy unto Abraham." When giving God his all, Abraham did not keep Isaac in reserve. He did not withhold Isaac.

Paul is repeating those very words, words revered by his Jewish audience, and saying, "He did not even hold His own Son in reserve, but gave Him up as an offering for you. Is that not the proof that all He has is available to you? God has given you His all. Everything. Do you see, if He loves you so completely that He did not even spare His own Son, could He possibly be reluctant to give you any other thing?"

Wholehearted God. Always fully present to us. Now, Debby Akerman gives us this challenge: Are we fully present to Him? Are we wholeheartedly surrendered to Him? Is there any part of our lives that we are holding in reserve and labeling, "Mine. All mine"?

Debby hits the nail on the head when she asks us to consider what it means to be wholehearted in our love and devotion to the One who is wholehearted in His love for us. Her clear writing, insightful scriptural teaching, and her obvious wholehearted love for the Father will draw you to pursue Him with your whole heart, nothing held in reserve.

PREFACE

ONCE YOU HAVE HEARD the voice of God speak into your heart with near audible words, your life will never be the same. Prayer will be more focused on listening to God than talking to God. You will long for more of those intimate moments of hearing His near audible voice. At times you will wonder if you remember the sound, the timbre of His voice. Rest assured, when you next hear holy God speak, it will be with immediate recognition.

Samuel heard God's voice call his name in the night. Do you think Samuel ever forgot the sound of his own name called out by God? Do you think Isaiah ever forgot the vision and the audible call of God: "Whom shall I send? And who will go for us?" (Isaiah 6:8). No. For when God speaks to us with a voice audible only to our ears and our heart, it is a pivotal moment on our spiritual timeline.

My spiritual timeline begins at the age of eight when I heard the call of God on my heart to believe in Jesus as my Savior through repentance of sin. God's call to me was compelling and propelling, sending me from the pew to the front of the chapel to kneel with my camp leader and ask Jesus into my heart. As a young woman, I heard God speak to my heart a call to recommitment to Jesus as my Lord. That morning in prayer, I heard God's voice say, "Come home." This second pivotal moment began a series of times I would hear from God in prayer, through Scripture, and even in the everydayness of my life.

Early on, God sensitized my heart for missions. The testimony of a missionary at my childhood summer camp primed my heart to hear God's call to salvation. After recommitment to Jesus as Lord of my life, God called me to serve as a leader in a children's missions group at church. This time God spoke three words into my prayertime as I prayed for a new leader for our daughter's missions group: "You do it." That would not be the last time I heard those three words from

God as I prayed. Each time they would be directed at serving Him in missions and through missions organizations at my church and other churches.

Walking with the Lord through life and through the Scriptures is a joy, as is discovering the intimacy of His presence and the richness of His Word. My study Bible is marked with dates that remind me of the pivotal moments on my spiritual timeline, times when I heard God speak to my heart, moments God marked with Scriptures that would take me deeper in relationship with Him and further in serving Him with a missions lifestyle—to the point of living wholeheartedly for Him.

INTRODUCTION

❧❧

*J*OURNALING THE WORDS   God speaks to me through Scripture and through prayer is part of my morning routine. For many years, with the Holy Spirit as my guide, I have worked my way through various books of the Bible verse by verse, selecting a word theme, such as gentleness or wait, to study. Whenever a new WMU® emphasis book was introduced, I focused on that theme in the Scriptures. I have a closet full of journals of all shapes, colors, and sizes, each containing precious moments of conviction, revelation, and direction from God.

Working my way through the Old Testament a number of years ago, I read a verse that had not before caught my attention: "But because my servant Caleb has a different spirit and follows me wholeheartedly, I will bring him into the land he went to, and his descendants will inherit it" (Numbers 14:24). Actually, this verse stopped me in my tracks as the Holy Spirit prompted the question, Do I have a different spirit? Quickly followed the question, Do I follow Jesus wholeheartedly? These questions are written in the margin of my Bible. These questions began my search for the secret to wholeheartedly following the Lord, of having an identifiably different spirit like Caleb, and of living in a way we could describe as "all for You—surrender, sacrifice, and serve."

We find these all-for-You elements depicted in the words of Jesus: "Then he called the crowd to him along with his disciples and said: 'Whoever wants to be my disciple must deny themselves

[surrender] and take up their cross [sacrifice] and follow me [serve]'"
(Mark 8:34). We, as Christ followers, know about serving, and we
seek to serve the Lord with our best ideas and energy. When serve is
spoken in the same breath as surrender and sacrifice though, we may
pause and reevaluate our serving. Does our serving flow from a totally,
every nook and cranny, surrendered heart and mind? Is our serving
strengthened as we lay all on the altar as a living sacrifice for Christ?
Do we, like Caleb, have an identifiably different spirit for serving our
Lord and Savior Jesus Christ?

Through stories of biblical, historical, and contemporary
missional men and women who have lived or are now living all-for-
You lives, Jesus' call to surrender, sacrifice, and service will resonate
with us. We can understand and apply His calling in our lives. These
stories will point to the personal need to take our Christ following to
a higher, holier level in wholeheartedly living for God.

Tommy Moore, who is a student minister at Ocean View Baptist
Church, Myrtle Beach, South Carolina, gives us a preview with a story
about what it means to discover wholehearted living:

I felt from a young age that God wanted to use my life, that the
circumstances surrounding my exposure to Him were far too odd and
complicated to be anything otherwise. I feared that one small misstep
or miscalculation in my pursuit of His destiny for me would sideline
the entire affair. That thought was terrifying. I was plagued daily with
visions of arriving at the end of my life defeated, forced to conclude
that I hadn't done anything remarkable, that I had wasted my existence and squandered my time. To me, there could be no worse fate.

Driving home from college one day, I had an epiphany of sorts,
a grand realization that was as real and as tangible as an actual light-
bulb going off over my head. Maybe God had called me to something
great—something greater than me. Maybe God had called me—
maybe God calls each of us—to join in the story of His glory,
a glory that started long before we got here and will continue long
after we leave.

I realized my own glory was far too small a thing to live for. Living
for my glory was making me vulnerable to necessary risks and forcing
me to weigh every option, to agonize over every minute detail, and to

live a life full of calculations, negotiations, fear, and anxiety. I would never know with any degree of certainty whether I had done enough, chosen correctly, or made the right move.

But living for God's glory, a much greater thing by far, involved laying down my life in complete surrender to Him. I realized the only way I could arrive at the end of my life with no regrets, with no feelings of defeat or nothingness, would be to die to my own life now and be resurrected in His, living a surrendered life that allows Him to live through me.

Now let's start at the beginning.

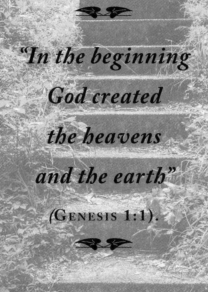

"In the beginning
God created
the heavens
and the earth"

(Genesis 1:1).

CHAPTER 1

Creative Love

NOT TOO FAR ALONG in our Christian pilgrimage, most of us can quote Genesis 1:1: "In the beginning God created the heavens and the earth." Whether we are brought up in the church or come to Christ in our later years, most evangelicals are creationists, believing God literally created the heavens and the earth, all that is in them, and humankind in His own image. Some of us may have pondered various points in the first two chapters of Genesis, also confronting various scientific theories presented to us in the secular world to confirm, with the Spirit's guidance, our belief in God's creation of heaven and earth. Regardless of whether we have gone through this exercise of confirming our beliefs, we may have missed the overtones of God's creative love.

God's original plan for His creation: an eternal, on-earth life in an all-with-Him relationship. Out of love for mankind our triune God envisioned and spoke into being all creation. Strong vocal tones often accompany the reading of Genesis 1, reflecting the creative speaking power of our almighty God: "Let there be light"! (v. 3). It is sometimes read with amazement at the creative results of God's commands: "And there was light!" (v. 3). And sometimes when we read the Creation story aloud to those hearing it for the first time, it is with the strength of a firm belief in its truth.

Take a few minutes to read Genesis 1 and 2 aloud in different tones—with tones of creative love in your voice. Yes! Please stop here and read it. Read each verse with a voice of love—with the tones you use when you talk to the ones you love most. Use the tones of love you used if you spoke words of promise to a future mate, if you first held your newborn child and spoke into that tiny heart, or when the love of Jesus Christ washed over you and you gave your heart to Him.

Now do you hear the love of God for all of His creation? Do you hear His love for the day and the night, for the sky and the earth, for the land and the sea, for the plants and the trees? Do you hear His love for the sun, the moon, and the stars; for the fish, birds, and the animals? God not only saw it was good, but He loved the results of His creative work! Listen for the love tones in God's voice that seem to say, Look what we have created; look how beautiful the earth is, and everything in it. Listen as He says to Himself, to His three-in-one Person, and says to His heavenly audience of angels, "This is good!"

From God's heart , He created His first child of God, Adam, and placed him in a perfectly good world. And out of Adam, He created the perfect woman, Eve. What a love event creation was! Holy God formed Adam from the dust of the ground. I ask myself, Did God, as He created man in His image, stoop down and cup His hands to lift the rich soil of earth? Did God compress and shape the soil to create one human part at a time until every system, every organ, every limb, every feature was just right and ready to function at the breath of God? We don't know. We do know that Adam stepped into a life that was perfect inside and out.

Imagine Adam as human life pulsed through his fully grown man body at the breath of God—a body that did not need to learn to walk or talk, a body that would be ever young and healthy, a body created for pure and eternal living in a heart and soul relationship with God. Did Adam, I wonder, take a panoramic view of his world before opening his mouth suddenly to speak his first words, echoing His Creator-Father, "This is good!"?

When we imagine hearing the voice of God pronouncing, "It is good!" the word good is given higher meaning. How casually we use the word good each day. When asked how we are doing, we respond with a colloquialism: "I'm good. Hope you are." At the store's check-out counter the words Have a good day drift our way as we pick up our purchases. These everyday goods are not the good of Genesis 1. God's good is an arms-spread-wide pronouncement of the vista of all creation. God's very good (v. 31) is man at the center of creation and in the center of His heart.

Adam was created with an innate heart for God, a soul-deep desire to be in right relationship with God, and yet with a will of his own. In Genesis 1, Adam lived in a degree of intimacy with God that would never be known again this side of heaven. Adam was taken by God to a new place to be responsible for the environment, taken to tend the Garden of Eden. Adam listened as God set boundaries for living, giving him the do's and don'ts of perfect living, and as He explained the penalty of death for committing the only must-not of garden living. Adam named all the birds and the animals as God brought them to him. Yet in all creation, there was none suitable to be his helper, his life companion.

Therefore, God created woman while the first man slept. God brought her to the man. It is said that the response of Adam is a song:

"This is now bone of my bones
and flesh of my flesh;
she shall be called 'woman,'
for she was taken out of man."
(GENESIS 2:23)

You have got to love a man who bursts into song at the sight of his bride. Adam, who was experiencing the love of God and his reciprocal love for God, began to experience a new God-given love, the love of man for woman. Ah! Life was perfect in the garden, just as God had planned for Adam and Eve.

What happened? What ended this perfect garden living? You know the story. Sin walked in as a serpent, speaking crafty doubt-casting words, luring the perfect couple with calculated lies to sin against God. Immediately their eyes were opened, and shame filled their hearts and souls, shattering their relationship with God.

Imagine the frantic minds of Adam and Eve, aghast at their shame, as they floundered in their new condition of lost innocence and attempted to cover their nakedness, which moments before had been a symbol of their purity. Imagine the all-new terrible feeling of fear gripping their hearts as peace seeped away, knowing God would soon come walking in the garden and see their shame.

God, in His great love for His created man and woman, made a way for them to be forgiven, to have a redeemed relationship with Him. One of the most tender, loving moments in man's history came after Adam and Eve sinned, after God sought them out, after He confronted their sin and pronounced the sin penalties. Seeing their attempts to cover their shame with leaves that would wither and die, revealing their sinful shame over and over again, God sacrificed one of the very animals named by Adam, cared for by Adam, to make coverings for their shame. God could have spoken a word, and they would have been clothed. God could have made their skin become a fabric covering. But God chose sacrifice as the way for sin to be forgiven, shame permanently covered, and souls to be redeemed—freed from the death-penalty consequence of sin, won back, restored.

God Himself made the garments of skin for Adam and His wife (Genesis 3:21). Picture with me God preparing the animal skins, providing Adam and Eve clothing that would signify forgiveness for sin and redemption by God in life after expulsion from the Garden of Eden.

And so began their need to be in right relationship with God, in a wholehearted relationship with God. God gave His people leaders and laws, prophets and promises—but in the end, it took the perfect sacrifice of the Lamb of God, Jesus Messiah, to provide perfect redemption.

Fanny Crosby wrote the timeless words our hearts sing when the sacrifice of Jesus on the Cross works in our lives to redeem us and make us a child of God: "Redeemed, how I love to proclaim it! / Redeemed by the blood of the Lamb; / Redeemed thro' His infinite mercy, / His child, and forever, I am."

Redemption in Christ Jesus is what paves the way for all-for-You living; it is what leads to heart, soul, and strength obedience to the key tenet of the Old Testament, "Love the Lord your God with all your heart and with all your soul and with all your strength" (Deuteronomy 6:5), and to the keeping of the Greatest Commandment as stated in the New Testament, "Love the Lord your God with all your heart and with all your soul and with all your mind" (Matthew 22:37).

APPLICATION

❧ Meditate on the word *redeemed*.

❧ Let the assurance of God's redemption flow through your heart and mind.

❧ Write out how you will live today as you love God with all your heart, soul, mind, and strength.

SECTION 1:

Surrender

"Love the Lᴏᴏᴄ your God with all your heart and with all your soul and with all your strength"

(Dᴇᴜᴛᴇᴏᴏᴏᴋ 6:5).

CHAPTER 2

The Wholehearted
Theme
of Scripture

I LOVE A THEME. With more than 30 years of planning for yearlong activities for a missions organization and special age-level and churchwide events, and with nearly as many years planning for organizational annual meetings, age-level trainings, and retreats, I don't think I have ever planned without an evident theme. As children's leaders in our little church, we created a missions theme when one was not provided and planned our year around it. Themes help us see the overarching purpose, the core values to adhere to, and the outcomes to achieve. I would contend that the theme of all Scripture is Wholehearted Love. Follow this theme with me from creation to revelation.

As God called the elements of the world into being, His love was present. At the time Adam and Eve hid in shame for their sin, God called to them with love. At the time 40 years of wilderness wandering would end for the Israelites, God called His people to love Him, the Lord their God, with all their heart, soul, mind, and strength. During the time of Jesus' ministry, He echoed those words, referred to as the Shema. At the time Christ took His last breath on the Cross for the sin of mankind, He called out in love, "It is finished" (John 19:30). Since time began and until time is no more, God's call of love to us is unequivocal. And this call reverberates to Him—in our wholehearted, all-for-You living.

Moses was chosen to all-for-You living in a rescue plan for God's people (see Exodus 1–4). Moses' mother took great risk in hiding her new baby after his birth. Although Moses was at least the third child born to Jochebed and Amram, the child was beautiful in his mother's eyes, as is the case since time began: "She saw that he was a beautiful child" (Exodus 2:2 NKJV). Consider, too, another version of that verse: "She saw there was something special about him" (*The Message*). Perhaps the "something special" about this new son was something God was revealing to Jochebed's heart about her child, something that caused her to risk her family's lives by desperately hiding her newborn so he would not be thrown immediately into the Nile.

We don't know what means she used to hide him. We do know that when he could no longer be hidden, she put her three-month-old baby son into a tar-and-pitch-coated papyrus basket and put it among the reeds along the side of the great river, trusting God with his life. With this rocking vessel, Moses' journey began toward an all-for-You life of surrender, sacrifice, and service for God.

Moses' journey is the stuff of which books have been written and movies made. It is a journey costumed children have acted out in plays for hundreds of years in churches and synagogues. This is a story that speaks to us today in our own journeys to live whole-heartedly for God.

Like Moses, we may have been rescued as a child from the dangers of life but did not find saving faith in our home. We may have fled our homeland out of shame for sin in our lives. Like Moses, we may have encountered God in our adult years and heard His voice call us to serve Him in ways we could not comprehend. And like Moses, we may be a leader of a people who struggle to stay true to God's command and to Jesus' affirmation to love God wholeheartedly, "Love the LORD your God with all your heart and with all your soul and with all your strength" (Deuteronomy 6:5).

MEN AND WOMEN WITH HEARTS FOR GOD

Many have argued whether DAVID was worthy to be called by God "a man after my own heart" (Acts 13:22). David's life has been scrutinized almost as closely as Jesus' life. Critics of David have zeroed in on the record of his blatant sins and tipped the scales of truth away from God's pronouncement, "a man after my own heart." Paul reaffirmed King David's wholehearted quality in the Antioch synagogue, saying, "God testified concerning him: 'I have found David son of Jesse, a man after my own heart; he will do everything I want him to do'" (Acts 13:22). *The Message* reading Bible presents God's affirmation of David with these beautiful words: "He's a man whose heart beats to my heart, a man who will do what I tell him."

JOHN THE BAPTIST was an all-for-You man of God. From before he was miraculously formed in his mother's elderly womb, he was known by God and set aside by God for kingdom service. His first moment of surrender to the lordship of Jesus the Christ came perhaps even before he was born, when newly pregnant Mary, with Jesus in womb, visited John's mother-to-be, who was in her sixth month of pregnancy (Luke 1). As the women greeted each other, yet-to-be-born John leaped in his mother's womb. Did John leap within his uterine cradle to a kneeling position as he was filled prenatally with the joy of being in the presence of his Lord?

ELIZABETH AND MARY are women who, like Jochebed before them, birthed men whose call to wholehearted living changed the course of history. We would love to have heard the conversations Elizabeth and Mary spoke about their God-authored pregnancies—as they shared their hopes and their fears for future years.

Questions about JOHN'S AND JESUS' early years arise too. Did they share feast times together as family; did they travel together to Jerusalem each year for the Passover? Did they study the Scriptures together as they each became *bar mitzvah* ("son of the commandment"), proceeding through this liturgical rite of passage while discovering and wondering at the prophecies concerning their own lives?

JOHN surrendered to God's call early in his life, choosing to be ready when God called him to precede Jesus' ministry by preparing His people for the imminent ministry of the Messiah. John also sacrificed many comforts, choosing desert living over a home in town, camel hair clothing over priestly robes, and locusts and honey for his meals over the traditional Jewish menu. John was a man who may have seemed wild, but he served God wholeheartedly.

Sent to "prepare the way for the Lord," as prophesied by Isaiah (40:3), John preached repentance for sins to the throngs of people who surged from Jerusalem and the whole Judean countryside (Mark 1). John spoke to them of the coming Messiah. Although John was baptizing them with water as a symbol of their repentance and forgiveness from God, he said the more powerful one coming after him, the Messiah, would baptize them with the Holy Spirit.

As John's ministry days came to an end in the prison of Herod the tetrarch, Jesus proclaimed John as the greatest of all persons born on this earth: "I tell you that no one ever born on this earth is greater than John the Baptist" (Matthew 11:11 CEV).

THE FULL CIRCLE OF ALL-FOR-YOU LIVING

The Apostle John also led an all-for-You existence. He began his Gospel writing with the most stunning of all beginnings of the books of the Bible since Genesis: "In the beginning was the Word, and the Word was with God, and the Word was God" (John 1:1). One can spend hours on this truth.

Jesus called this John and his brother James to leave their nets, follow Him, and become fishers of men. Three years later, the Cross of Calvary looming, John was at Jesus' side during the Last Supper. John described himself as "the disciple whom Jesus loved" (John 13:23; 21:7, 20). Jesus loved all His disciples, but it was into John's care that Jesus, from the Cross, entrusted His devoted mother (John 19:26).

It was to John that the vision of heaven opened. It was John who heard and recorded the last of Jesus' words to us of what is to come. It is easy to see why this all-for-You disciple, often now called the Revelator, felt so beloved. The Book of Revelation is a call to surrender in faith to the lordship of Jesus, to sacrifice all to be a faithful follower of Christ, and to serve the Lord so "persons from every tribe and language and people and nation" will know they have been purchased by the blood of Jesus Christ, to be part of the kingdom of God (Revelation 5:9).

APPLICATION

❧ How does the theme of wholehearted living for God, as demonstrated by men and women throughout Scripture, cause me to examine my heart of love for God?

❧ Am I living all-for-You for my Savior, Jesus, for the almighty God, who is and was and is to come (Revelation 1:4)?

"But because my servant Caleb has a different spirit and follows me wholeheartedly, I will bring him into the land he went to, and his descendants will inherit it" (Numbers 14:24).

CHAPTER 3

Caleb Had a
Different Spirit

❧❧

ALFHEARTEDLY FOLLOWING JESUS? Not me! Or
so I thought until I read the following Scripture: "But
because my servant Caleb has a different spirit and follows
me wholeheartedly, I will bring him into the land he went to, and his
descendants will inherit it" (Numbers 14:24). In the margin of my Bible,
I wrote these questions: Do I have a different spirit? Do I follow God
wholeheartedly? This began my search for the secret to wholeheartedly
following the Lord, of having an identifiably different spirit, and of
living in a way in which I can say to God, "All for You."

More questions came to my mind: What did Caleb experience
in relationship with God that I had not experienced? What did Caleb
know that I did not know? With Christ in me and me in Christ on
this side of the Cross, should I not be able to plumb the rich depths of
Scriptures to discover the essence of Caleb's spirit and wholeheartedness? God opened my heart to this understanding as I began to study

His Word, focusing on passages with the word wholeheartedly and the phrase all your heart.

God's desire is for us to delve into His Word so deeply that the Word, as a two-edged sword, pares away layers of spiritual self-satisfaction and reveals to us the all-for-You life.

The outcome of Caleb's wholehearted following of God is clearly evident in Scripture:

"Now then, just as the Lord promised, he has kept me alive for forty-five years since the time he said this to Moses, while Israel moved about in the wilderness. So here I am today, eighty-five years old! I am still as strong today as the day Moses sent me out; I'm just as vigorous to go out to battle now as I was then."
(JOSHUA 14:10–11)

Because Caleb had a different spirit, he had complete trust in God's power, promises, and purposes and was able to wait through 40 years of wilderness wandering for his entry to the promised land. Because Caleb followed God wholeheartedly, he was able to see with visionary eyes and hold on to what God had promised. And because Caleb lived in an all-for-You relationship with God, the Lord preserved his strength and vigor for experiencing God's promise.

TAKING GOD AT HIS WORD

Caleb's resolute story of taking God at His Word and believing the promise of God for the future is not so much a story of a man with great faith, but of a man of faith in a great God. What knowledge birthed his faith? What experiences sealed his faith in a great God? I believe Caleb's coming to know the presence, provision, and protection of God during the Exodus from Egypt led him to wholehearted faith.

Did he daub the blood of a sacrificed lamb on the top and sides of his doorframe before the angel of death passed over? Did he gather his family and his belongings to join the Israelite throng following their new leader Moses? Did Caleb find his faith growing in this journey through the faithful presence of Jehovah God, who, in a pillar of cloud by day and a pillar of fire by night, guided them? Was there a leap of faith in his soul as he watched Moses lift his staff, stretching it over the waters of the Red Sea, the waters parting: "The LORD drove the sea back with a strong east wind and turned it into dry land. The waters were divided, and the Israelites went through the sea on dry ground, with a wall of water on their right and on their left." (Exodus 14:21–22)?

For two years, Caleb experienced the protection and provision of Jehovah God and the leadership of Moses. He would have eaten the daily portions of manna and drunk the water from the rock. He would have been there when Moses walked up Mount Sinai and received the law. Did he see Aaron succumb to the pressures of some of the people wanting a god, an image they could worship? Did he, resolute in growing faith, stand back and turn his back on the sin with Joshua, Moses' young aide?

Was Caleb watching from a distance when the original stone tablets with God's law etched into them by God's finger crashed to the ground from Moses' hands at the sight of idolatry? Could he later, from the crowd of hundreds of thousands of men, not to mention the women and children, see the freshly etched tablets of stone as Moses presented the law of God, his face radiant from having been in the presence of God on the mountain? Did Caleb's faith take new steps on that day to follow God and His law wholeheartedly?

HE WILL DIRECT YOUR PATH

God was at work all through Caleb's life: in Egypt, in the wilderness with Moses, and in the promised land. God was at work, too, in the lives of Bob and Susan Brindle as they followed Him wholeheartedly along a 40-year path, serving God together as North American Mission Board missionaries in New England. Susan, now retired, reflects on their experience:

"In all your ways acknowledge Him, and He shall direct your paths" (Proverbs 3:6 NKJV). This was a familiar verse, one Bob and I had both memorized as children, probably as participants in . . . the missions organizations that nurtured our missions service "calls." This verse was embedded in our hearts and on our minds. As adults, there came that call to wholehearted surrender that would redirect our lives—His call to serve in northern New England. Could He really be directing our path to such a distant outpost of service? Could we really trust Him in this difficult decision? We would be so far away from our families. Life there was so unfamiliar. It would surely be difficult and perhaps even lonely knowing no one there.

These thoughts flooded our minds and mingled with the fresh thoughts of sheer excitement knowing God was at work in a place that seemed so distant. A church had been birthed in Vermont, the very last of our 50 states to have a Southern Baptist church. A small congregation was there worshipping in a carriage house and waiting for a pastor and his family. God had already given us a glimpse of what He was doing in New England. A few Southern Baptist churches had been established in the great Northeast corridor, and I had visited to lead conferences in some of those churches.

Our minds could not begin to grasp the vastness of the task. There were so many people, so many towns, and so few churches of any denomination in that region. We would be leaving a loving, fast-growing new church in Maryland, with strong and capable leadership. Why would we want to leave when God was now blessing us so richly?

Our struggle to surrender to this new call continued. Answering the call didn't make sense if we looked at the list of pros and cons, but this is not how God works. His strong Word says, "Trust in the Lord with all your heart, and lean not on your own understanding" (Proverbs 3:5). Our pros and cons list could not be trusted. Our trust must be placed fully in Him who had always led us and would continue to lead and guide our ways.

Forty-six years have passed since that first big step of surrender in faith and in trust. Was it, at times, a struggle? Yes. Was it, at times, difficult? Yes. Yet it has been an amazing journey that has allowed us to see God at work over and over again. We have witnessed the "new birth" of many precious New Englanders. Churches have been planted in the great cities and the small villages across the six-state region. We were privileged to participate in that growth.

Just as God planted churches in New England, He planted a deep-rooted love in the hearts of our family for this region of America and the folks here. What may have seemed to some to be a difficult place of ministry has been for us a life of rich blessing and grateful trust in the Holy One, whom we serve.

Six years ago, God completed the task He had given Bob and gave him a new heavenly assignment. Bob's earthly body is buried here in New England soil, the place we have so loved and where He planted our hearts!

GOD AT WORK IN OUR LIVES

God is at work in our lives, too, and provides evidence of His presence, protection, and provision. Think of a time in your life when God made a way of escape from a situation that threatened to enslave you, a time like Caleb's in Egypt before the great Exodus. Was it an addiction that enslaved? Drugs, alcohol, pornography, gossip, or gambling can enslave and make our living for Christ halfhearted—we know Him but don't live for Him. When release is found in God's leading out of bondage and His protection is felt day and night in new freedom, faith grows.

Now think of a time in your life when the path ahead of you in following the Lord seemed impossible. Was it like an unbridgeable Red Sea barrier to what God wanted for you, a barrier that suddenly opened for you, with a clear path that enabled you to pursue His plan for your life? Was it the college God was leading you to attend, the career path God showed you, the place God wanted you to live, the children God promised you, or, like for the Brindles, the missions field God beckoned you to enter? It is true what Don Moen's lyrics say, "God will make a way / Where there seems to be no way." When God makes a way, faith leaps.

And finally, think of a time when crowd mentality threatened your heart and soul, which you had once given to the Lord. Was it to set aside the boundaries of God's law to embrace the ways of the world that were so enticing? Was it to succumb to the pressures of others and go along with the cries of the crowd even though, as the leader, you knew this would not please God? Were you able to walk away from the revelry of wrong living? When we take steps in resolute faith and do not succumb to sin, we are really taking Caleb-size steps of faith to follow God and His law wholeheartedly. When we take a stand faith flourishes.

APPLICATION

❧ Describe a time when God's presence to protect and provide impacted your life.

❧ What list of pros and cons do you need to set aside to surrender to God's call?

❧ What Caleb-size steps of faith do you need to take to live an all-for-You life?

"Then Caleb

silenced the people

before Moses and said,

'We should go up and

take possession

of the land, for we

can certainly do it'"

(Numbers 13:30).

CHAPTER 4

A Minority Voice Reveals a Whole Heart for God

❧❧

NOTHER QUESTION PRESENTED ITSELF as I studied Caleb's life: What did Caleb experience in relationship with God that I had not yet experienced? Joshua is named among the Israelites as an aide to Moses (Exodus 24:13; 33:11; Numbers 11:28). But no mention is made of Caleb until the Canaan exploration party is selected (Numbers 13:6). During the two years' travel from Egypt to the Desert of Paran, many events served to increase Caleb's knowledge of God. But what personal experiences actually validated this knowledge?

Taberah is the place where God's fire burned in anger against the complaining Israelites (Numbers 11:1–3). It may have been for Caleb the site of an extraordinary experience with God. Moses was feeling the burden of leading these often-complaining, rabble-rousing refugees. He was at the end of the proverbial rope and asked God to do him the favor of putting him to death. God seemed to ignore Moses' death plea. Instead, God presented a plan for the leadership to be shared with 70 others, leaders and elders known to Moses among the people—in other words, 70 respected and faith-filled leaders from the 12 tribes. We know that Caleb, at age 40, was considered a leader, as he was the one leader from the tribe of Judah soon to be chosen by Moses to go on the Canaan scouting expedition. Was Caleb also one of the 70 leaders chosen to share in Moses' leadership? Was he one of the leaders who stood at the tent of meeting with Moses and experienced God taking of the Spirit resting on Moses and placing it on them? Was Caleb one of the 70 who, upon experiencing the Spirit resting on them, prophesied? Since that gathering, it appears Caleb had been helping to carry the burden of leading the Israelites, for God said Caleb had a different spirit.

As mentioned previously, this was an exploratory party. The Israeli 12 were about to embark on 40 days of exploring Canaan. (By the way, 40 days is a significant span of time for those who follow God wholeheartedly. God sent rain on the earth for 40 days and nights while obedient Noah and his family and all created pairs of species were in the ark. Moses had been on Mount Sinai with God for 40 days. We should not put too much emphasis on the number, except to be sure to pay attention when it shows up. In the span of 40 minutes in God's Word or in prayer, or 40 days and nights of waiting for Him or serving Him in some way, or sometimes even 40 years of life in the desert or in delightful days, God has experiences for us that will grow our faith into all-for-You living.) On their return from 40 days of exploring and discovering the challenges, as well as the richness of God's promised land, 10 men, the majority of the explorers, acknowledged the richness but brought a negative report, a terror-producing report. Their eyes were focused on the fortifications instead of the force of God's power. Their minds were focused on their fear of powerful giants instead of reverent fear, obedient fear of Almighty God.

BOLD VOICE OF THE MINORITY

Caleb, however, spoke boldly and positively to the people: "Then Caleb silenced the people before Moses and said, 'We should go up and take possession of the land, for we can certainly do it'" (Numbers 13:30). According to another version, "Caleb calmed down the crowd" (CEV). Still other translations use the word quieted (NASB, for example). Caleb, saying, "I know we can do it," was the voice of reason, as well as the bold voice of the minority that interrupted the pessimistic voices of the naysayers. He spoke with assurance that they could do exactly what God had promised because he had experienced God in Canaan, seeing the promised land as God saw it.

I am personally persuaded by Caleb's report; at least, today I am. If not convinced in that initial moment, I like to think I would have been by that night when, in a near mob scene, the people clamored for a new leader and wanted to return to Egypt. But would I have been persuaded then? Do I today have that different spirit to take a stand with the minority voice?

To these fearful, rebellious, and irrational people, Caleb, along with Joshua, stepped up and encouraged the people to go for it:

"The land we passed through and explored is exceedingly good. If the LORD is pleased with us, he will lead us into that land, a land flowing with milk and honey, and will give it to us. Only do not rebel against the LORD. And do not be afraid of the people of the land, because we will devour them. Their protection is gone, but the LORD is with us. Do not be afraid of them."
(NUMBERS 14:7–9)

Great speech! Caleb identified their two problems, fearfulness and rebellion. They often go hand in hand. Possibly many wanted to believe them and did not want to return to Egypt at all. However, fear conquered reason, and rebellion broke out. "The whole assembly talked about stoning them" (Numbers 14:10). Have you ever wondered, What is wrong with these Israelites? as you read their history in the Old Testament? Probably we all have at one time or another. This event is one of those times. "Then the glory of the LORD appeared at the tent of meeting to all the Israelites" (v. 10). From His glory, God condemned the ten who incited the rebellion with their fear-provoking report. However, about Caleb, He said, "But because my servant Caleb has a different spirit and follows me wholeheartedly, I will bring him into the land he went to" (v. 24).

The Israelites' refusal to obey God, refusal to go in and take the land, resulted in God punishing them with 40 years of wandering in the wilderness, 1 year for each of the 40 days the 10 rebellious spies explored but then failed to trust God. God ordained that none of those who treated Him with contempt, grumbling against Him, would live to enter the promised land. For the ten who brought the bad report, God struck them with a plague.

On the other hand, Caleb's speaking out for God even though in the minority, a boldness produced from personal experiences with God, evidenced a different spirit that was willing to follow God wholeheartedly. God's plan for Caleb to sacrifice his young years wandering in the desert was rewarded with long life, as he outlived all his contemporary Israelites except Joshua, whom he would accompany into Canaan. Caleb, with an unaged body and mind, took the land awarded him through battles won in the strength of the Lord. God's identification of Caleb as His servant is what one day we trust we will hear in heaven when we see Jesus and He says, "Well done, good and faithful servant" (referencing Matthew 25:21).

IDENTIFIABLY DIFFERENT SPIRIT

Caleb-like people, men and women with a different spirit, have risen up in Christian history from time to time. CORRIE TEN BOOM is one who had a different spirit. Like Caleb, she followed God wholeheartedly. Corrie ten Boom and her family lived in full surrender to Jesus. They chose to express their faith in Christ and devotion to His law through peaceful resistance to the Nazis.

They sacrificed their personal safety during the Nazi occupation of the Netherlands, choosing to put their lives in God's hands. Betrayal sent this wholehearted family to concentration camps, but not before they had helped to save more than 800 Jews and protect many of the underground workers. They served God through hiding Jews and transporting them out of the country as the Gestapo relentlessly hunted down Jews for extermination. Like Caleb, they were the minority voice speaking out for God through their actions.

Corrie's different spirit kept her through separation from family, her horribly cruel Ravensbrück camp experience, and the death of her sister Betsie. Her whole heart for God enabled her to forgive her captors and her tormentors. With wholehearted compassion for others who had known the terror and torment of the camps, she established a home for camp survivors trying to recover from the horrors they had escaped.

If you think Caleb's and Corrie's times were different and their experiences do not apply to your average life, think again. It is into the everydayness of life that God calls us to all-for-You living. You may hear that call through the life of one who mentors you, one in whom you identify the spirit seen in Caleb's life and Corrie's. Their voices may well be the minority, accepting you into the family of faith when others dismiss you as one without potential. Their voices may encourage you to live in wholehearted surrender to God's future for you when others see only your past.

Susan Brindle, whose story you read in the previous chapter, has been my mentor and friend for many years. I knew from the first days of my relationship with Susan that she had a different spirit. When I was a new church member, she included me in fellowship with other women, introduced me to WMU and Southern Baptist missions, encouraged me when life burdens were heavy, and championed me as God called me to serve Him in specific areas of missions through WMU.

Like Caleb, Corrie, and Susan, we are to become men and women with identifiably different spirits—men and women who surrender, sacrifice, and serve wholeheartedly. I hope the following prayer attributed to Dr. David Jeremiah will help you.

Lord, today I surrender my life to You. I choose Your will to be done, not mine. I want to be closer to You, God, than I am to myself. I accept Your terms for my life today and purpose to live personally the crucified life, which I received positionally through faith in Christ. I ask You to give me grace today to be a surrendered soldier of the Cross.

APPLICATION

❧ Do you have a different spirit, one that is a minority voice outside mainstream Christianity?

❧ How do you think God describes your spirit today?

❧ Pray a prayer of surrender today and each day.

"Who do you say I am?"

(MARK 8:29)

CHAPTER 5

The Heart of the Matter

❧❧

ALEB AND CORRIE TEN BOOM experienced unexpected circumstances that redirected their lives, and lived devotedly for God. Caleb endured Israel's 40 years of wilderness wandering and whining. Corrie endured 10 months in the dreadful confines of a Nazi concentration camp. They did not deserve to suffer. Yet God's redirection of their lives gave them experiences that set each on a path for serving that honored Him. Perhaps you have experienced redirection in life.

The Gospel of Matthew presents the settings for redirection experiences for the first few of Jesus' disciples. Matthew describes a seashore setting to which I can relate, having lived most of my life near the seashore of New England. In these places, boats, fish, and fishermen were part of our stories' local color. The dockside fish market was supplied with the catch of the day from the returning fishing vessels. It was a frequent stop on my way home from work, its strong aromas evoking memories of visiting extended family on Cape

Cod who treated us to their own fisherman's catch of the day when we visited.

Matthew tells the story of Jesus' invitation to four fishermen to come follow Him in (4:18–22). The fishermen abruptly left their boats and equipment, proving how compelling Jesus' call to follow Him was. In all my experiences with the fishing community, professional and recreational, I have never witnessed fishermen simply walking away from their valuable tools of the trade.

In John 1:35–42, we read that at least Andrew and Simon Peter had spent time with Jesus, heard His preaching, and become spiritual followers of Him. They had heard the "Come and you will see" invitation from Jesus first. So when they heard Jesus' invitation, "Come, follow me, and I will send you out to fish for people," they pushed away from the practical and familiar and traded the fisherman's life to be retooled to be fishers of men.

Surrendering our all is leaving our nets at the sound of Jesus' voice to follow Him wholeheartedly. Full surrender empties our hands and our lives so they can be filled by the purposes God has for us.

CRITICAL QUESTION AT A PIVOTAL TIME

Jesus' interactions with persons met along dusty roads, in market-places, or outside temples resulted in spiritual teachings and personal questions that led His disciples to a pivotal moment recorded in Mark 8.

Jesus and his disciples went on to the villages around Caesarea Philippi. On the way he asked them, "Who do people say I am?" They replied, "Some say John the Baptist; others say Elijah; and still others, one of the prophets." "But what about you?" he asked. "Who do you say I am?" Peter answered, "You are the Messiah." Jesus warned them not to tell anyone about him. He then began to teach them that the Son of Man must suffer many things and be rejected by the elders, the chief priests and the teachers of the law, and that he must be killed and after three days rise again. (MARK 8:27–31)

Jesus' question, "Who do you say I am?" (v. 29) is the most important question ever asked. It was the critical question for those 12 men at a pivotal point in time. It evoked the answer that transformed them into Christ followers, taught them about cross carrying, and took them from the Calvary death into the Resurrection life of their Jesus, the Christ, their nation's long-awaited Messiah.

Join me in allowing these verses to simmer in our hearts and minds. Wonder with me what the atmosphere may have been among the disciples following their teacher that day. Put yourself in their sandals as Jesus first asked the group, "Who do people say I am?" (v. 27). It was not a difficult question to answer. They had heard many discussions on who Jesus was and were quick to answer. As the names of Elijah and John the Baptist were spoken, did a potential personal response come to the front of their minds or, more importantly, the midst of their hearts?

Jesus' words, "But what about you?" (v. 29), stopped them in their tracks. With this, Jesus got personal, asking, "Who do you say I am?" (v. 29). Did these 12 men, in their first steps of messianic faith, hear with Jesus' question the echo of Yahweh speaking to their ancestor Moses, "I AM WHO I AM" (Exodus 3:14)? Did the words of the prophet Isaiah about the coming of Messiah appear like a scroll unfurled in their minds (Isaiah 9:2–7)? Did their eyes move to Peter, the one among them known for so often being the first to answer Jesus' questions, wondering what brash answer he would give this time, wondering whether he would get it wrong again?

But Peter nailed it! In that moment, he knew. The answer rushed from his heart as, with an unwavering voice, he proclaimed into the waiting silence, "You are the Messiah" (v. 29). Those were profound, concise words from the former fisherman, soon to be fisher of men.

The Gospel of Matthew gives an expanded account, attributing Peter with saying, "You are the Christ, the Son of the living God" (Matthew 16:16 NASB). Matthew continues on with Jesus' response: "Blessed are you, Simon son of Jonah, for this was not revealed to you by flesh and blood, but by my Father in heaven" (v. 17).

WE, TOO, MUST MAKE OUR CHOICE

When God speaks into the pivotal moments of life with a critical question, He speaks with a clear voice that stops us in our tracks. His questions cause us to dismiss what others say, as did the disciples, evoking a personal search for a heartfelt response. With Jesus' question, "Who do you say I am?" the Spirit of God reveals the truth of God to the one in whom seeds of faith have been planted by those living a missions lifestyle.

C. S. Lewis, in his book *Mere Christianity*, addressed the issue of who Jesus is:

I am trying here to prevent anyone saying the really foolish thing that people often say about Him: "I'm ready to accept Jesus as a great moral teacher, but I don't accept His claim to be God." That is the one thing we must not say. A man who was merely a man and said the sort of things Jesus said would not be a great moral teacher. He would either be a lunatic—on a level with the man who says he is a poached egg— or else he would be the Devil of Hell. You must make your choice. Either this man was, and is, the Son of God: or else a madman or something worse.

If, like Caleb and Corrie ten Boom, we are to become men and women with an identifiably different spirit, men and women who surrender, sacrifice, and serve our Lord, we, too, must make our choice. The heart of the matter in all-for-You living is our response to Jesus' voice asking, "Who do you say I am?" Can you answer confidently with Peter, "You are the Christ, the Son of the living God"?

Surrender demands this declaration of who we believe Jesus is. We learn from Peter and Andrew the steps to surrender. Step one was taken as they laid down their nets first to go and hear the witness of John the Baptist. Step two was, on being pointed to Jesus, turning to follow Him. Step three of surrender was responding to the "Come and you will see" of Jesus; an invitation to move closer to Him and to discover new life in Him. Like Peter and Andrew, we must put down the nets of our everyday life to hear the truth of Jesus. Like the first disciples, we must turn from simply listening to the Word of God, to faithfully following the Living Word of God, Jesus. Then we will come close, see our Savior face-to-face, and walk with Jesus side by side. And so, we move toward wholehearted surrender.

I SURRENDER ALL

Judson W. Van DeVenter (1855–1939) was a successful teacher and administrator of high school art in Pennsylvania. He also studied and taught music, having mastered 13 different instruments, and was a singer and composer. He was part of his Methodist Episcopal church music ministry. After time, as a follower of Jesus, he found himself struggling for nearly 5 years between the comfort and success of his teaching career and the growing desire to be part of an evangelistic endeavor. In 1896, while conducting music for a church event, he finally surrendered his personal desires completely to God, making the decision to leave his nets and surrender his all to the Lord. It was in his surrender that a hymn was born in his heart, a hymn that has been sung for more than 100 years and has seen tens of thousands come kneel at the altars of our churches as they wept and sang "I Surrender All."

When we come to the altar in full surrender to the call of Jesus, as did Judson Van DeVenter, we may find ourselves weeping and singing that sweet hymn of submission:

> *All to Jesus, I surrender,*
> *All to Him I freely give;*
> *I will ever love and trust Him,*
> *In His presence daily live. . . .*
> *All to Thee, my blessed Savior, I surrender all.*
> *(Judson W. Van DeVenter, "I Surrender All")*

DOUG'S STORY OF SURRENDER

Today in Mexico, Doug and Darla Millar are serving God in wholehearted surrender. Doug's story began in a chapel service in seminary. A group of students, having just returned from a missions trip to Romania, shared their experiences of serving in a country emerging from 70 years under a Communist regime. The stories were amazing to hear, but Doug's reaction was not to pray, "Send me, O Lord." He remembers telling God, as he walked home, of his thankfulness to be part of a seminary and a denomination that send missionaries to places like Romania and saying to God, "I am so glad I don't have the $2,000 needed to go to Romania on the next trip because I don't have time." On arriving home, Doug opened his mailbox as his prayer ended. There he found a letter from the real estate company that handled the sale of their home two years previously; the letter explained a mistake made in the transaction. With the letter was a check for $2,280. With tears, he told his wife, Darla, he would be going on a missions trip to Romania in March. That two-week trip would change their lives forever.

Arriving in Romania, the team learned that the Communists had imprisoned and executed many in Romania for reading their Bibles. He listened to the stories of pastors' experiences with amazement at their faithfulness and God's provision in the face of severe persecution. Doug shared one pastor's story that has had a lasting impact on his life:

Pastor Tank (not his real name) was a Bible smuggler for most of his life, risking his life to bring the Word of God into Romania. One story he told us centered on his favorite passage in the Bible, Psalm 23. With the trunk of his car loaded with more than 300 Bibles, he crossed the border back into Romania. The penalty for bringing even 1 Bible into the country at that time was life in prison or even execution. There would be 11 checkpoints between the border and his house. When Pastor Tank came to the first checkpoint, he began to pray. God heard and answered his prayer. He was flagged through the first checkpoint. As he continued on, he became increasingly anxious with ten more checkpoints to get through. He pulled over to the side of the road to pray and cry out to the Lord. Getting out of his car, he walked out into a field where, through his tears, he saw a lake. It was there by the lake that God brought the encouraging words of Psalm 23 to his mind.

Returning to where he had parked, to his dismay, he saw a young army officer standing by his car; the officer asked for a ride. Not having an option, Pastor Tank said, "OK! Get in." Pastor Tank's anxiety mounted as they approached the next checkpoint. They were flagged straight through, no questions asked. The same was true with the nine remaining checkpoints. This officer may have been God's angel for Pastor Tank that day.

My life was changed as I heard this story and understood that where God calls you He will make provision. I knew in that moment

God was calling me and Darla to cross-cultural missions. And I knew if God was calling us, He would provide, just as He had for Pastor Tank. For the first 10 years in Mexico, we were supported by the International Mission Board (IMB). In 2005 we were asked to relocate to a new mission site. We had started a new church in the Yucatan of Mexico, and things were going well as we ministered to the emerging middle class in Playa del Carmen. We knew God had called us specifically to these people and the work was just beginning. We faced the dilemma of continuing with the organization in a new missions assignment or continuing with God's call on our lives to the people we were serving. Staying would mean losing our monthly support as well as our house, car, insurance, and funding for our two children in college. With only $1,500 in savings, how could we stay?

I thought back on all the missionary stories I had heard about trust and faith, and I thought about men like Pastor Tank. I don't have the words to tell you all the miracles that God has done since we chose to stay on the Yucatan Peninsula, but He worked it all out in amazing ways. Seventeen years later on the missions field in Mexico, we are praising God for His faithfulness to provide for all our needs. God is great!

APPLICATION

❧ Picture yourself in the fishermen's shoes as they were about their everyday work. Has Jesus watched as you mended your nets or cast your life's nets again and again, busy with the everydayness of life, not seeing the lost around you?

❧ Have you heard His call to come and follow Him in a new life that will reequip you to share His love with others? Describe the call.

❧ What will it take for you to surrender all the nets you hold on to so that you may follow Jesus wholeheartedly?

*"Be careful not to forget
the covenant of the
LORD your God
that he made with you;
do not make for
yourselves an idol in the
form of anything the
LORD your God
has forbidden.
For the LORD your God
is a consuming fire,
a jealous God"*

(DEUTERONOMY 4:23–24).

CHAPTER 6

Do Life the Deuteronomy Way

NINE TIMES MOSES used "all your heart" language in his Book of Deuteronomy to exhort the Israelites to live in right relationship with their Jehovah God. Nine times Moses called the people of God to rededicate their lives so they would be strong to resist the pagan worldview they would encounter in the promised land they were poised to enter. Nine times Moses recorded "all your heart" guidance for us to do life the Deuteronomy way.

Deuteronomy tells of Moses' words warning the Israelites against pagan worship of idols. With the promised land in view and battles to be waged and won in the strength of the Lord, Moses wanted God's chosen people to be spiritually pure as they went into battle. Moses, having been raised amid the gold and silver images in Egypt's polytheistic culture, warned them at length. He knew Israel's pattern of sinful conformity to the prevailing worldview that worship was best at the feet of shiny manmade idols.

Be careful not to forget the covenant of the LORD your God that he made with you; do not make for yourselves an idol in the form of anything the LORD your God has forbidden. For the LORD your God is a consuming fire, a jealous God.
(DEUTERONOMY 4:23–24)

He went on to remind them of the severe punishment for past failure to resist this temptation, to remind them of the destruction that would come if they succumbed to pagan worship. These were hard words for those who at Baal Peor stayed true to Jehovah God and had not perished in God's wrath at Israelites worshipping Baal (vv. 3–4).

Moses ended his sermon call to renewed commitment with a personal word of knowledge of God's grace for any failure in their commitment to God, saying, "But if from there you seek the LORD your God, you will find him if you seek him with all your heart and with all your soul" (v. 29). Moses wanted them to know—as God wants us to know today—that He, the almighty God, tolerates no god before Him in our lives. When we set up idols before Him in our lives, even idols not made with human hands but whatever the world deems more important than a relationship with God, God's discipline will follow. But we will not be eternally doomed. Christ Himself has paid the penalty for sin. God provided a promise of restoration if we seek the Lord our God, if we look for Him with all our heart and with all our soul.

THE SHEMA

The Shema is a Jewish confession of faith that begins with a passage from Deuteronomy 6 in which Moses, per God's instruction, acknowledges the Lord God is one and commands whole-being love for Him:

Hear, O Israel: The Lord our God, the Lord is one. Love the Lord your God with all your heart and with all your soul and with all your strength.

These commandments that I give you today are to be on your hearts.
Impress them on your children. Talk about them when you sit at home
and when you walk along the road, when you lie down and when you get
up. Tie them as symbols on your hands and bind them on your foreheads.
Write them on the doorframes of your houses and on your gates.
(DEUTERONOMY 6:4–9)

Living life the Deuteronomy 6 way begins with seeking the Lord with all our heart in repentance and renewal by His grace. Only then can we experience triune love for our triune God. Only then can we declare with verse 4, "The LORD our God, the LORD is one." Only then can we choose to obey the command of verse 5, the heart of this declaration, "Love the LORD your God with all your heart and with all your soul and with all your strength." God the Father gave His people the Shema that would stand forever and become the greatest commandment from the mouth of God the Son (Mark 12:29–30). God desires and deserves to have all our love, wholehearted love.

John later wrote a truth begun in Creator God's heart: "We love him, because he first loved us" (1 John 4:19 KJV). Our love for God will never be as deep or as wide or as complete as God's love for us. But if we focus on God's great immeasurable love, if we take time to bask in God's unconditional love, and if we open our eyes to see all the signs of God's love for us in our lives already, our hearts will choose to respond with wholehearted love for Him.

Wholehearted love is a choice. With this choice comes the choice to obey the word God speaks into our hearts. Moses presented the choice the Israelites had to make: "And now, Israel, what does the LORD your God ask of you but to fear the LORD your God, to walk in obedience to him, to love him, to serve the LORD your God with all your heart and with all your soul" (Deuteronomy 10:12). Just as Moses spoke God's words to God's people, God speaks to us through godly people, Moses-like leaders. He speaks through these same Deuteronomy words to us today.

These are words from God that cannot be ignored. They call us to surrender through wholehearted love and obedience. God never forces us to love or obey Him. He asks us to choose. The key word is ask. God asks us to respond to His love, giving us heart and soul choices. He asks us to fear Him in reverential awe rather than reject Him for idols of the world. He asks us to walk in His ways in godliness rather than stray down the road of godlessness. And He asks us to serve Him out of love rather than serve self in rebellion. There is no middle road, no fence we can straddle in wholehearted love for God.

William Wilberforce and John Newton were contemporaries in eighteenth-century England. John Newton, best known as the author of the beloved hymn "Amazing Grace," was a renowned preacher, prolific writer, powerful prayer warrior, and composer of 270 published hymns. God placed him on a mentoring path with William Wilberforce to accomplish His purposes.

Wilberforce, having read many of Newton's writings and having sat under his preaching, sought out Newton for spiritual guidance. Wilberforce struggled with knowing God's will for his life—whether to stay in parliament and wage the battle against the slave trade or to become a minister of the gospel. Newton's counsel comparing Wilberforce's place in parliament to Daniel's place in Babylon with King Nebuchadnezzar is what set Wilberforce on his life's path.

Rosa Lee, guest writer for the Christian Broadcasting Network website, wrote about the relationship between Wilberforce and Newton in a special feature:

Wilberforce and Newton shared more than a conversation; they shared heart knowledge of time spent running from God looking for freedom and happiness in evil places. Yet, both came to understand that true freedom and joy lie within the immensity of God's unending love and grace. They considered themselves unfit for God to use, yet surrendered their lives to His plan, to be used in the manner that God preferred.

PROMISED LAND LIVING

Deuteronomy 11 continues the wholehearted theme with promises, provision, and prerequisites for God's chosen people.

But the land you are crossing the Jordan to take possession of is a land of mountains and valleys that drinks rain from heaven. It is a land the LORD your God cares for; the eyes of the LORD your God are continually on it from the beginning of the year to its end. So if you faithfully obey the commands I am giving you today—to love the LORD your God and to serve him with all your heart and with all your soul—then I will send rain on your land in its season, both autumn and spring rains, so that you may gather in your grain, new wine and olive oil. I will provide grass in the fields for your cattle, and you will eat and be satisfied. Be careful, or you will be enticed to turn away and worship other gods and bow down to them.
(DEUTERONOMY 11:11–16)

First, God promised them a land to be their home—a place He had created, made fertile, watched over, and intended for them. Second, God provided the land with perfect seasons for rain, growing, and harvesting. God provided the land with fields of green grass and meadows for grazing livestock. God provided satisfying harvests that would always meet their needs. Finally, God presented three prerequisites for this blessed life in the promised land. The first, faithful obedience to God's commands, then wholehearted loving and serving God, followed by being careful to never turn away from God to pagan gods.

These promises from God to His chosen people in the final days of 40 wilderness-wandering years seem to apply to His chosen people of today—some who are still wandering, still seeking the promised land of a life fully surrendered to God.

Like the Israelites then, some Christians live today enslaved by sin, dying a bit each day in servitude to sin's hold on their lives. Out of fear, they do not take the last step of surrender to God's lordship of their lives. Living with one foot pointed toward the world and one foot toward God, they overlook the pain of their hearts and soul and attempt to find peace and joy in life outside the promised land. They find themselves directionless in today's worldview version of wilderness.

Promised land living is found only in wholehearted surrender to the lordship of Jesus Christ. In personal surrender, all who enter the promised land find the mountains and valleys of real life, but also experience God's faithful promises, His protection, and His satisfying provision there; they experience the peace and joy found only in Jesus.

REFINING FIRES IN THE PROMISED LAND

Living with an all-our-heart and all-our-soul love for God will not be without times of challenges—times allowed and times presented by God for refining our love and surrender to Him. The Israelites were forewarned, in Deuteronomy 13:1–5, that if they heard a voice calling out to them of miraculous signs and wonders, calling them to follow a deceptive path to the altars of other gods, they must not listen to those words. They were to stay true to the voice of truth, the voice of God spoken through His true servant Moses.

The LORD your God is testing you to find out whether you love him with all your heart and with all your soul. It is the LORD your God you must follow, and him you must revere. Keep his commands and obey him; serve him and hold fast to him.
(DEUTERONOMY 13:3–4)

In producing the finest gold, a refining fire is needed to remove the dross, the extraneous substances that reduce gold's value; so, too, God will allow us to experience the crucible of refining fire to live continually in surrender to Him. The heroes of faith named in Hebrews 11 lived through God's refining fire: Noah in an ark, his family the lone survivors of a world-changing flood; Abraham, on a mountain with knife in hand, ready to slay his only begotten son on an altar; Joseph, sold into slavery in Egypt with dreams yet to be fulfilled; Moses, daubing the doorposts with the blood of a sacrificial lamb as the angel of death approached; and Rahab, trusting in the scarlet cord of faith as the walls of Jericho came tumbling down around her. As a result of enduring and surviving the refining fire, these heroes of faith saw life through the lens of deeper surrender to God.

Today, some persons call their personal experience with God's refining fire a *crisis of belief.* This term was expanded on by Henry Blackaby in his Bible studies, *Experiencing God: Knowing and Doing the Will of God* and *Called and Accountable: Discovering Your Place in God's Eternal Purpose.* Blackaby showed us, through Scripture, how a crisis of belief comes when God asks us to surrender anew to join Him in what is beyond our abilities and our proclivities, in what is far outside our current understanding of God's call on our life, to find His will, way, and to obey.

Just as the Hebrews' Hall of Faith Old Testament heroes experienced crises of belief, so, too, have many New Testament individuals who became heroes of faith. Mary, the soon-to-be mother of Jesus, said to the visiting angel Gabriel, "May your word be fulfilled" (Luke 1:38). The Samaritan woman who met Jesus at the well returned to her town with this announcement: "Come, see a man who told me everything I ever did. Could this be the Messiah?" (John 4:29). Stephen, as the stones rained down on him, prayed, "Lord, do not hold this sin against them" (Acts 7:60), echoing the words of his Lord on Calvary. Peter surrendered as he heard Jesus ask for the third time, "Do you love me?" (John 21:17. And then as blinding light flashed around Saul, later known as Apostle Paul, he fell to the ground and called out, "Who are you, Lord?" (Acts 9:5).

And this is also true of you if you have surrendered your life to the lordship of Jesus Christ and have taken up your cross daily to follow Him wholeheartedly, choosing to love with Shema love, loving the Lord with all your heart and with all your soul and with all your mind. This is true of you if you have allowed the refining fire of God to prepare and equip you to serve Him wholeheartedly.

The historical Book of Deuteronomy nears its end with the powerful heart and soul admonishment by Moses to God's people in chapter 30. These verses picture the wholeness of life, the holistic blessed life of walking in God's ways, loving God with all one's heart and soul. These verses recapture the importance of repentance from sin to God, restoration of relationship with God, and renewal of commitment to God. With these verses, Moses gave his final call to wholehearted surrender:

"This day I call the heavens and the earth as witnesses against you that I have set before you life and death, blessings and curses. Now choose life, so that you and your children may live and that you may love the Lord your God, listen to his voice, and hold fast to him. For the Lord is your life."
(DEUTERONOMY 30:19–20)

APPLICATION

❧ Describe a time you experienced God's refining fire in your life and evaluate the outcome.

❧ What crisis of belief has challenged your wholehearted surrender to God?

❧ What soul repentance and heart renewal are needed to live steadily and wholeheartedly for God?

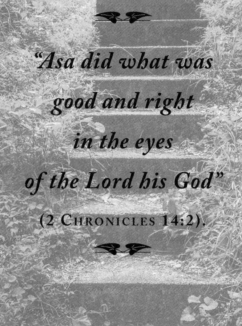

"Asa did what was

good and right

in the eyes

of the Lord his God"

(2 Chronicles 14:2).

CHAPTER 7

King-Size Wholeheartedness

❧❧

D O YOU HAVE A GOOD NUMBER of days when your surrender quotient feels pretty high—days you sail through with a "bring it on" attitude toward all who cross your path, call your phone, or connect with you through the Internet? I do, and I even have strings of days when my surrender feels wholeheartedly king-size. Long meetings, delayed flights, and late hours writing in my study fail to sap my strength. At the end of those days, I feel poured out, not used up; that feeling is oh so good.

In reality, I am not wholeheartedly surrendered every hour of every day to God's call on my life. Some days I want to lay down the cross of wholehearted serving I picked up that morning in my quiet time. I want to put off returning calls and emails, put down the files, and close the computer. Even as I write this paragraph, I am distracted by the close proximity of our beautiful white, sandy beaches on the coast of South Carolina and the invitation to sit under my friend's umbrella, sharing a day of sunshine and ocean breezes. Why not just go and write tomorrow, you ask? My answer is this: Because today was set aside for writing, because today God answered my prayer and is feeding my heart and mind with words to be written.

As we think about king-size wholeheartedness, we realize this concept goes far beyond the individual incidences of the particular activities of our days and weeks and beyond the temptation to enjoy playing hooky at the beach now and then. This speaks to living life at an all-for-You level of commitment to God and withstanding the temptations to set it all aside and settle for less.

Parents of a physically handicapped child know the day-in and day-out compassionate caring demanded of them to meet special needs. Soldiers deployed to war zones know the 24/7 readiness and alertness required to fulfill their military commitment. And kings of biblical renown knew that the rise and fall of their kingdoms rested on their ability to rule the people justly and to win the battles against the enemy. A look at a few kings will help us see how they achieved king-size surrender and dealt with the temptations to set aside the responsibilities that come with wholehearted living.

GOOD KING ASA

Asa was one of Judah's good kings. "Asa did what was good and right in the eyes of the LORD his God" (2 Chronicles 14:2). The verses that follow recount the godly deeds of Asa's reign. He tore down everything that was not pleasing to the Lord and led the nation to live in obedience to God's laws. When God granted years of peace to Judah, Asa wisely built up the kingdom to stay strong and alert for when battles would come. When attacks from Judah's enemies came, King Asa prayed to the Lord, his source of empowerment to fight the battle.

King Asa's reign presents three points for us to consider: remove offense, rest and retool, and pray.

First, King Asa removed items of offense to God, such as foreign altars and high places where false gods were worshipped. We must tear down anything in our lives that is not pleasing to God. As a young wife and mother, I belonged to a popular book club. Each month I looked forward to the selection arriving in the mail. During my daughter's nap time, I would immerse myself in romance or intrigue, escaping a bit from the reality of toilet training, toy-strewn rooms, and toddler conversation. Some of the books made me a tad uncomfortable with their themes of scandal or evil, but not uncomfortable enough to set aside the books. One morning in my quiet time, as I read Scripture about living a pure and unblemished life, my eyes strayed to the bookshelves that were filling up month by month. Scripture seemed to be pointing a holy finger at some of those books and saying to beware of the subtle influence those books would have on my life. This experience was a reminder that to have a godly home, our home must remain free of the things that are offensive to our Lord. One by one, I looked at them to see which ones must be discarded because they were inconsistent with a life lived surrendered in obedience to Jesus Christ.

Second, King Asa made use of times of rest to fortify the nation and to foster prosperity. When God brings us times of refreshing—physically, mentally, and spiritually—we should use the times wisely. Our lives need respite from work and responsibility. In those times, we refuel and retool to serve the Lord with renewed commitment. And we all know, even God rested on the seventh day.

Finding a church and places in which to serve the Lord figured high on our to-do list as my husband, Brad, and I moved to Myrtle Beach, South Carolina, from New Hampshire. The first church we visited resulted in a visit from the pastor. As we sat in our family room, he asked the expected what and why questions regarding our move. We enjoyed telling him of our full life back north and our hopes for our new life here. How surprised we were when he quietly offered this advice: "I believe God is giving you this time to rest and be refreshed. He does have purpose for you here, but now is the time for rest. Don't hurry to decide on a church or to take on responsibility. That will come."

We took his wise advice. We joined a gym and conditioned ourselves physically. We read the local papers and explored our new community and surrounding area. And we spent large amounts of time in prayer, personal Bible study, and reading some of the books we had not had time to read before. Soon enough, God showed us the church He wanted us to join, the church responsibilities He would have us take on, and the ministry we were to share. God had prepared us in our time of rest and peace to better serve Him.

Third, King Asa prayed when the battle began. He knew he was powerless and that God was his power source. He knew that he could only meet the enemy head on if he relied fully on God and went into battle in the name of God.

Myrtle Beach has become a retirement destination. In our cul-de-sac of eight homes, all built at the same time to welcome new families, only two of the homes were purchased by families with children and local employment. The rest were bought by retirees from various states. Some retirees came for the golf, some for the beach, and all for the lack of snow. Some sought out places to volunteer, some looked for part-time jobs, and some looked for groups in which to share their hobbies. We, too, were seeking purposeful activity, and God led us into a battle, a battle for souls.

Behind the beach stores and seafood buffets is a subculture of homeless people. Street Reach, the local faith-based homeless shelter with an in-house Christian addiction-recovery program, is where Brad and I began serving two years after our arrival here. Seeing this shelter as a place we could show Christ's love and mercy, our commitment began with twice-a-month singing and speaking from God's Word at the nightly mission service. It grew into a king-size commitment of weekly Bible studies, support groups for persons who had relapsed, and Christian 12-step groups.

As time progressed, Brad's responsibilities increased. His reliance on Jesus to cover him in the armor of God (Ephesians 6:10–18) for the battle against evil for souls has also increased. God has armed him to stand firm with the belt of truth, presenting Jesus as the only high power for sobriety. God has readied him to mingle with the residents, wearing the boots of the gospel of peace and the breastplate of righteousness, to interact with lives that have no peace or right living. With the shield of faith, his personal faith in Jesus, and the sword of the Spirit, which is God's Holy Word, he is daily prepared to enter spiritual battle in the name of God for the souls of men and women. Many in recovery at Street Reach have come to Christ and gone on to live wholeheartedly for God because men and women with king-size wholeheartedness have done battle for their souls.

GOOD KING WENCESLAUS

Other than a few words from a seldom sung Christmas carol, most of us know little of this Christmastide man called King Wenceslaus. Wenceslaus was indeed a king and a good king reigning over the country of Bohemia, contemporary Czech Republic, more than 1,000 years ago. We sing of his pious faith and deeds, which are true. According to Gene Fedele in his book, *Heroes of the Faith*, young Wenceslaus was educated by his grandmother and, from her, learned to love God. "She taught him that faith has to be put in action or it is not genuine," Fedele wrote. "Because of her teaching and example, Wenceslaus learned true concern for the poor and suffering." Although his reign as king was short, it was marked by his wholehearted love for God, reformation of the country's judicial system, reduced oppression of peasants by the nobility, peace with neighboring nations, and his urging of fellow Bohemians to become Christians. He reminds us a bit of King Asa. Good King Wenceslaus was martyred at age 28 by his heathen brother and other rebels, as they seized control of the kingdom.

This Christmas when you sing of good King Wenceslaus, think about his wholehearted love for God. And as you sing the last few words, "Therefore, Christian men, be sure, / Wealth or rank possessing, / Ye who now will bless the poor, / Shall yourselves find blessing," think of demonstrating your wholehearted love for God with genuine deeds of faith.

KING JESUS

Matthew and Mark both wrote of Jesus' conversation with an expert in the law discussing which is the most important of the Old Testament commandments. In these accounts, we see the beginning of the Shema presented by Jesus as the most important of the commandments from the Old Testament:

Jesus replied: "'Love the Lord your God with all your heart and with all your soul and with all your mind.'
This is the first and greatest commandment."
(MATTHEW 22:37–38)

"The most important one," answered Jesus, "is this: 'Hear, O Israel:
The Lord our God, the Lord is one. Love the Lord your God with all
your heart and with all your soul and with all your mind
and with all your strength.'"
(MARK 12:29–30)

The importance for us in these incidents is how they serve as proof texts of Jesus' incarnate purpose to fulfill the Law, the recorded spoken words of God to Moses, as the Living Word of God among men.

I wonder as I reflect on the Gospel writers' reports whether Jesus' Son of man words resonated with His Son of God heart. Were these words a reflection of His triune part of God speaking these words to Moses on the mount so long ago? Were these words commingled in response to years as a young Jewish man learning Torah and participating in the worship and rituals of their faith? And finally, I wonder if it was pure joy for Jesus to proclaim this truth, affirm this command from the mouth of His Father God to love the Lord God with all our hearts, souls, minds, and strength.

King Jesus spoke about this wholehearted love for God and how wholehearted surrender is the key to this degree of love from a personal perspective. In John 4, after Jesus' conversation with the Samaritan woman at the well, His disciples returned with food and urged Jesus to eat, holding back their questions about seeing Jesus talking with the woman. Jesus responded, "I have food to eat that you know nothing about" (v. 32). Then He explained: "'My food,' said Jesus, 'is to do the will of him who sent me and to finish his work'" (v. 34). The food Jesus was referring to is the word for nourishment, spiritual nourishment. The act of serving others in word and deed nourished Jesus on this long three-year journey to Calvary. Our God nourishes us in many ways: through Bible study, prayertime, worship, and serving others who are lost without Jesus. If our spiritual diet has only the first three, we will become nutritionally imbalanced. We will be vessels who have been filled up but have not been poured out in the work of the Lord.

APPLICATION

❧ What commonalities do you see in the wholehearted love for God demonstrated by King Asa and King Wenceslaus?

❧ What have you learned from King Jesus' surrender to His Father's will that can guide you to wholehearted surrender to your heavenly Father?

SECTION 2:

Sacrifice

"And whoever
does not carry their cross
and follow me
cannot be my disciple"

(LUKE 14:27).

CHAPTER 8

Counting the Cost
of Carrying the Cross

⟨decorative ornament⟩

LL-FOR-YOU LIVING IS A CHOICE as well as a command
from King Jesus. Listen to the voice of Jesus as recorded
in Mark 8:34, watchword for us: "Whoever wants to be my
disciple must deny themselves and take up their cross and follow me."
Whoever of the Twelve would choose to be a follower of Jesus must
surrender, sacrifice, and serve. Whoever from that point in history
would choose to be a follower of Jesus must make a cost-counting
choice, not an impulsive choice, and must completely eliminate all else
to follow Jesus.

"Whoever wants to be my disciple must deny themselves and
take up their cross and follow me" were startling words to the 12
men who had so recently heard their brash fisherman friend Peter
proclaim Jesus as Messiah and Son of the living God. These words
were a wakeup call to the disciples, who perhaps had nodded their
heads in agreement with Peter when he proclaimed Jesus was the

Christ. These were deflating words to any ballooning thoughts of how this Jesus, Messiah, would restore Israel to Solomon's days of might and glory and to ideas of how they as disciples would have prominent places in the restored kingdom, which they expected would be soon to come.

Was Peter alone as he spoke against Jesus' new teaching that He would not reign on earth now but instead would suffer and die (Mark 8:31–33)? Or were the disciples again nodding their heads at Peter's rebuke of Jesus' teaching, stepping up and into agreement with Peter? Did they back away from Peter as the eyes of Jesus swept across each one of them, knowing the track of their imaginations, as Jesus' words of rebuke were finally directed at Peter? Into the postrebuke hush comes Jesus' call to the crowds to listen with the disciples to His words of cross-carrying discipleship.

Crucifixion was the most dreaded and disgraceful form of execution by the Romans in the days of Jesus' ministry. The sentenced criminal was first severely scourged and then forced to carry his own crossbar to the crucifixion site, a sign of submission to Roman rule and a warning to the observers that they too must submit to Rome's authority. The cross carrier's hands and feet were then nailed, or in some instances tied, to the cross to await an agonizing death. The disciples and all in this crowd following Jesus would have borne witness to crucifixion. None in the crowd wanted to hear about this degree of cost to discipleship. But Jesus put it right out there for all to consider. Following Him would have not only its rewards but also its serious life-threatening risks.

This reference to a cross was not the only one in Jesus' teachings. Jesus spoke clearly about counting the cost of being His follower to crowds traveling with Him in Luke 14:25–33. He called for the same cross-carrying degree of surrender in verse 27: "And whoever does not carry their cross and follow me cannot be my disciple."

With this second cross-carrying statement, Jesus launched into analogies for counting the cost of being a disciple. Using real-life issues of His day, He compared this with a builder's need to accurately estimate the costs for his construction project so that he would not only start well, but would build on the foundation with confidence and complete the structure with integrity. He added to that the considerations a king must make as he weighs the risks and rewards of engaging in battle, the realistic evaluation of manpower against the potential for loss of life. Jesus did not want anyone to make an impulsive emotional choice to believe in Him as the Son of God. Jesus wanted those who followed Him to be aware of the risks and the rewards of following Him as they counted the cost of carrying the cross in a no-turning-back decision.

Consider with me Jesus' words in Luke 14 together with His words in Mark 8:35–37: "For whoever wants to save their life will lose it, but whoever loses their life for me and for the gospel will save it. What good is it for someone to gain the whole world, yet forfeit their soul? Or what can anyone give in exchange for their soul?" With those words, life and death would forever hang in the balance for anyone considering being a disciple of Jesus.

Jesus wants all to give full consideration to the risks and rewards of following Him and not to make impulsive decisions that will not last.

I HAVE DECIDED TO FOLLOW JESUS

Jesus wants us to make a complete, no-turning-back choice. Not until Jesus was crucified did the 11 remaining disciples fully understand His cross-carrying references. They could think back and remember how Jesus turned His holy face toward Jerusalem and the Cross and did not turn back. Until their own deaths, they would remember how Jesus became their example, carrying His own cross to Calvary. They would count it a privilege to give up their life for the cause of Christ. Traditions handed down through the centuries tell us all the disciples but John were martyred for their faith.

The Apostle Paul gave us the application of spiritual crucifixion when he wrote to the churches: "I have been crucified with Christ and I no longer live, but Christ lives in me. The life I now live in the body, I live by faith in the Son of God, who loved me and gave himself for me" (Galatians 2:20). "For we know that our old self was crucified with him so that the body ruled by sin might be done away with, that we should no longer be slaves to sin" (Romans 6:6).

Cross-carrying surrender began to mark the identity of those who chose to be Christ followers as persecution gained momentum against the early church. *Cross carrying,* like today's descriptive *card-carrying* phrase, denoted full commitment to the cause and full participation in its work. Jesus' call to the crowd was to count the cost of surrender, to prepare to sacrifice their lives, and to serve in full participation in the cause of Christ, with no turning back.

Remember your moment of salvation—your moment of moving from lost in sin to saved by grace as you asked Jesus to forgive your sin. For many of us, those born-again moments were in response to an invitation to come forward and pray with the pastor or a counselor. My moment of salvation was at summer Bible camp. I remember the music as the chapel service ended and the invitation was given. My footsteps going forward might well have been in sync with the rhythm of the familiar chorus, "I Have Decided to Follow Jesus," because it was at camp that I first sang those words. Ever since, I have equated the song with surrender to Jesus as Savior and Lord.

According to the Global Christian Worship website, the hymn "I Have Decided to Follow Jesus" comes from India with the lyrics based on the words of a mid-nineteenth-century Christian convert who was martyred for his faith. When the village chief demanded he renounce his faith, it is said he responded, "I have decided to follow Jesus." To threats to his family's lives, he said, "Though no one joins me, still I will follow." The story continues with his wife being killed and his execution as he sang, "The world behind me, the cross before me." Today's hymn form is attributed to Indian missionary Sadhu Sundar Singh.

Knowing the origins of this hymn as we sing it helps us understand in the moments of the most important decision we will ever make that deciding to follow Jesus is not just following the crowd or even your friends in some comfortable life improvement plan. It is leaving your worldview for a view of Calvary. It is cross-carrying surrender even if none go with you. It is no-turning-back, denying surrender of self to the lordship of Jesus Christ no matter the cost, saying with Paul, "For to me, to live is Christ and to die is gain" (Philippians 1:21).

NO TURNING BACK

God wrote another song on the heart of a modern-day cross-carrying young woman in the Middle East. The following is her story as told to me by a Christian worker involved in international ministry:

I was traveling in the Middle East and met a young woman who had come to faith in God from a Muslim background and community.

In a place where the gospel is new and there are no churches and few Christian resources, the Spirit of God sometimes uses dreams and visions to prepare hearts for the gospel and to strengthen the faith of new believers in the face of persecution. This song is one such example of how the Spirit of God moves. The woman who first sang this song had been detained by the police for her "Christian activities." She was interrogated for several hours, threatened with prison and worse. At one point she told me that she was placed alone in a holding cell in the basement of the police station for several hours. There was only total darkness, no light. She heard small animals in the cell, but could not see them. She felt along the walls and floor with her hands and found only a dirt floor and earthen walls. As terror began to overtake her in that place she said that she felt a warm glow in her heart. The Holy Spirit of God began to bring words to her mind and she began to sing this song.

Yarub Asma' Shakwati ("O Lord, Hear My Troubles")

> *Lord, hear my troubles,*
> *Lord, hear my troubles,*
> *Lord, have mercy on my tears.*
> *No one but You can save me.*
> *I have no father, I have no mother*
> *(who can save me).*
> *I have no sister, I have no brother*
> *(who can save me).*
> *You are my light in the darkness.*
> *Within these four walls, have mercy on me.*
> *My room is dark, but You are my light.*
> *You are the light in my heart.*
> *You are sufficient for me.*
> *Save me! Save me, O my Lord.*
> *O my Lord, give the judge fear and anxiety because of me.*
> *O Lord, give the judge terror and anxiety from you.*

She said the song gave her assurance that her heavenly Father was with her and she was no longer afraid.

What this young woman did not know was that the police interrogator heard her as she sang. He went down into the basement and opened her cell door and ordered her back into the interrogation room, demanding to know where she had learned this song. She told him that God gave it to her. He ordered her to sing it again. At one point, he became visibly shaken and upset and had to leave the room. He asked her if he released her, would she stop telling people about Jesus. She declared that she would not stop. Finally, after making further threats, he agreed to release her. Because of the late hour, he actually drove her home! On the way to her home, the policeman who had interrogated and threatened her told her about a problem he was having with his young daughters who were terrified of the dark. He actually asked the woman if she would come to his home and teach her song to his young girls so that they would no longer be afraid of the evil spirits. This young believer has continued to face harsh persecution for her faith and has suffered great difficulties. Two weeks after I met her, she was again detained, but this time she was severely beaten. In spite of this, the work of the Lord has continued to spread.

APPLICATION

❧ What cost consideration has been part of your Christ-following journey?

❧ How do these no-turning-back stories impact your cross-carrying life in Christ?

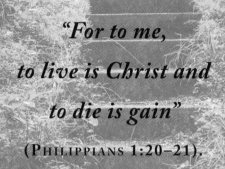

"For to me,

to live is Christ and

to die is gain"

(Philippians 1:20–21).

CHAPTER 9

Upright Living in an Upside-Down World

L OW ON THE TWENTY-FIRST CENTURY'S LIST of desirable attributes for man sits the character trait of surrendered. Surrendered has never been the most desirable attribute in any century. Synonymous with surrender are terms such as *give up, admit defeat, yield, abandon, forfeit, submit,* and *lose.* All these terms strike a negative tone with which men's and women's hearts struggle. Our cultural vocabulary has been filled with winning sayings that have shaped this predominant worldview. Artist Vincent van Gogh said, "Winning isn't everything...it's the only thing." Dianne Feinstein, US senator from California said, "Winning may not be everything, but losing has little to recommend it." Leo Durocher was described in one obituary as "perhaps major league baseball's best example of the win-at-all-costs manager." He was attributed with saying, "Show me a good loser and I'll show you an idiot."

Be it the arts, politics, or sports, surrender is not part of today's vernacular. Winning is lauded. Surrender is booed. Wholehearted followers of Jesus find themselves striving to live upright in an upside-down world and to live surrendered to the biblical worldview of Jesus.

All-for-You living says with John the Baptist, "He must become greater; I must become less" (John 3:30). The King James Version of the Bible says it this way: "He must increase, but I must decrease." John the Baptist knew from the womb that his role would be to point others to Jesus, no matter how many he baptized, no matter how many followed him in his ministry. You may be a leader in your church, your missions organization, or your Bible study. You may be a leader in your association, your state, or nation. No matter where you lead, the truly surrendered life always points to Jesus.

And all-for-You living says with Paul, "I eagerly expect and hope that I will in no way be ashamed, but will have sufficient courage so that now as always Christ will be exalted in my body, whether by life or by death. For to me, to live is Christ and to die is gain" (Philippians 1:20–21).

Long ago I copied this prayer from a now forgotten source: "God, may I abandon so much of self that Jesus is who people see."

Abandon self. Surrender self. Die to self.

FROM THE TOP DOWN

With all this in mind, it is time to adjust our lenses to see the world as Jesus did: three-dimensionally and intrinsically. This is the worldview God has given us through Scripture.

Jesus viewed the world in the first of three dimensions literally from the top down on several occasions. In Luke 4:1–13, Satan took Jesus to a high place and showed Jesus the kingdoms of the world and tempted Jesus to embrace his evil worldview. Jesus looked down with holy resistance, knowing He was to be the Savior of the people in those same kingdoms. In Matthew 5:1–2, Jesus appears to look down from the mountainside with compassion on humanity crowding at his feet, and He began to teach what we have named the Sermon on the Mount. And then finally in Luke 23:34, as Jesus was crucified, He looked down from the Cross on Golgotha, looked down with mercy and love from His agony and degradation, looked down at the soldiers and others gaping at His impending death, and asked His Father God to forgive them for they did not know what they were doing. Jesus saw the world from the top down!

So what is up with that? How can we have a from-the-top-down view like Jesus? An acronym from a past decade challenged us to have a biblical worldview: WWJD (What would Jesus do?). Before that, several generations ago, the novel *In His Steps: What Would Jesus Do?* by Charles Sheldon influenced many to live a biblical worldview. A from-the-top-down worldview is truly about having the mind of Christ, which T. W. Hunt wrote about *(The Mind of Christ: The Transforming Power of Thinking His Thoughts).*

We can have a from-the-top-down view like Jesus' if we learn from His examples. From His temptation experience, we can learn how to resist the temptation to want more control and more of the seeming splendor of that which is of the world. We can become content with the authority, possessions, and places of service God has given us. From Jesus' mountainside experience, we can learn that there is great lostness of the world, at our doorstep, across our land, and in every people group of the world. And from Jesus' last words on the Cross, we can learn that by loving those who continue to thwart the gospel—from the neighbors or co-workers who criticize, to radicals of other faiths who persecute the church, to politicians who enact laws that uphold principles contrary to God's Word—we live surrendered to the will of God.

FROM THE BOTTOM UP

The second dimension of how Jesus viewed life is from the bottom up. Jesus said to His disciples, "Anyone who wants to be first must be the very last, and the servant of all" (Mark 9:35). In the Sermon on the Mount, Jesus said, "Blessed are the meek, for they will inherit the earth" (Matthew 5:5). And then again to His disciples, Jesus said, "Whoever finds their life will lose it, and whoever loses their life for my sake will find it" (Matthew 10:39). So what is up with that? And what is the application for our worldview? I believe the key point is meekness, a hallmark of the holiness of our Lord Jesus.

Jesus' Mark 9 conversation with His disciples is about them not getting too big for their boots. As a nurse, I eventually reached nurse-manager level; in that position, I had opportunities and even encouragement to do just that—get too big for my boots. One incident that stands out in my mind is when a bedpan, doctor rounds, and my supervisor collided with my view of nursing. While making rounds with a surgeon and an internist, a patient called from behind the curtain of a four-bed ward, "Nurse, can you pleeeeease help me?" Checking on her, I discovered she had been left long on a bedpan without being able to remove it herself or reach her call button. Immediately, I attended to her needs and then caught up with the rounding doctors in the next patient's room. Later the supervisor called me out for abandoning her priority of having the doctors' needs met while they made rounds, although they were just fine in the few minutes it took me to meet the patient's desperate need. The supervisor thought I needed to let a nurse's aide know the need when rounds were completed. I told her that I saw the patient's misery as more important than the doctors' need to have a nurse hold their charts. The supervisor did not like my response. However, the nurse-manager who had mentored me in my early years of nursing taught me to never think I was too important to take care of the patient's needs above all else. Jesus also taught us to put serving people first in Matthew 23:11–12: "The greatest among you will be your servant. For those who exalt themselves will be humbled, and those who humble themselves will be exalted." We must remember that although God exalts those who humble themselves, such a person is seldom exalted by the world.

The world has never liked the word *meekness*. It is the predominant characteristic of Caspar Milquetoast, a wimpy comic strip character created by H. T. Webster for his cartoon series *The Timid Soul*. Webster, probably the best-known newspaper cartoonist in the mid-twentieth century, redefined forever the word *meekness* for the prevailing worldview, describing his character Caspar Milquetoast as "the man who speaks softly and gets hit with a big stick."

Jesus' meekness, His holy surrender to His Father's will, flew in the face of the worldview when He walked this earth. He was more than hit with a big stick; He carried the cross He would die on. True meekness is letting God have control over our lives. Meekness is not lack of power, but rather empowerment by God to accomplish His will in our lives as we live an all-for-You life.

Find life; lose life (as described in Matthew 10:39). One commentary describes this as a positive and negative statement of the same truth: clinging to this life can cause you to forfeit the best from Christ in this world and the next. The more we cling to this life's rewards—possessions, power, popularity, financial security—the more we discover how empty these rewards are. Releasing our grasp on these things frees us to live wholeheartedly for Christ and to experience benefits of surrendering to a life of serving Him and eternal life as well.

FROM SIDE TO SIDE

Jesus had great peripheral vision. At the Last Supper, the disciples on either side of Him, He spoke final words to them and in humility washed their feet, modeling again His great love for them (John 13:1–17). On the Cross, in His own human agony, Jesus hung between two thieves. He hung there dying for both of them as well as for the world. He responded out of His godness and goodness and gave salvation to the one who believed (Luke 23:43). After Jesus' resurrection, we find Jesus walking along the road to Emmaus with two disciples who did not recognize Him (Luke 24:13–35). Can you picture them walking and shaking their heads as they related from a skewed worldview their disappointment in what had happened to the person they had hoped would be their Redeemer? Then Jesus, who is the Way, the Truth, and the Life, began to talk to them of Moses and the prophets. He told them the whole story, burning it on their hearts!

So what's up with all that? First, as Jesus washed the disciples' feet, He modeled for us the equality of believers. Jesus washed all 24 feet, even Judas's feet, knowing the steps of betrayal Judas would soon be taking. Jesus offered equal forgiveness for the disciples' equal sin status. Jesus gave them equal measures of the Father's love. We are to see each other in the family of God as equals, loving each other and serving each other as equals.

Second, Jesus, as He hung on the Cross, modeled for us "interruptibility." No matter what our day is like, God has the right to interrupt us—in our grief, in our suffering, in our joy, in our busyness, in our plans, in our leisure—to connect us with someone who is dying spiritually without knowing the Savior.

And third, Jesus, as He walked with the two to Emmaus, modeled for us a readiness to share the salvation story. We are to be ready to give our testimony of faith in Christ. We are to be ready to explain the Scriptures and to start at the beginning if needed. And we are to be willing to go the extra mile with those who do not yet understand.

FROM INSIDE OUT

Jesus always knows our hearts and our minds. Jesus knew those muffled sarcastic words of the Pharisees who sought to maintain their worldview and to silence Jesus' worldview. He knew what Martha was really upset about when she said no one was helping her in the kitchen

(Luke 10:38–42). Jesus knew the sin mind-set and heartache of the woman at the well (John 4:1–26).

So what is up with that? What do these familiar glimpses of Jesus' ministry mean to our worldview? Jesus provided the example of persistence in the face of resistance to the gospel. *Those Pharisees,* we wonder, *did they ever get it?* Some did because of Jesus' persistence. *That neighbor, or co-worker,* we wonder, *will they ever get it?* We are to be persistent, as was Jesus, with those who resist our Lord. Then Jesus gave us the example of patience and kindness for when we, too, face anger, resentment, and division among believers. How sad it is that we will likely, at some time, experience such disharmony. And finally, Jesus gave us His example of discernment and directness to get to the heart of the matter with sinners we meet on our journey. Can we, as Jesus did, discern their desperate heart's cry for love, mercy, and the forgiveness that only Jesus can give?

APPLICATION

❧ God is holding us accountable to live like Jesus did, by the world-view revealed through Scripture. Give examples of how you, in this upside-down world, will live an upright surrendered life as you share the gospel.

❧ The Apostle Paul wrote of relying on the grace of God for upright living: "We have conducted ourselves in the world, and especially in our relations with you, with integrity and godly sincerity. We have done so, relying not on worldly wisdom but on God's grace" (2 Corinthians 1:12). What Scriptures will you claim for living uprightly in this upside-down world?

"Teach me your way, LORD,
that I may rely on your
faithfulness; give me an
undivided heart, that I may
fear your name. I will praise
you, Lord my God, with all
my heart; I will glorify your
name forever. For great is
your love toward me;
you have delivered me
from the depths,
from the realm of the dead"

(PSALM 86:11–13).

CHAPTER 10

The Undivided Heart

"CROSS MY HEART AND HOPE TO DIE" is an idiom voiced by children on playgrounds. These words are often followed by the back-and-forth of "Did not" and "Did so." It is an oath promising the truth of a statement or of the telling of an event that others cannot believe. This idiom has application for us as we finish unpacking what it means to be fully surrendered to Jesus Christ in order to live wholeheartedly for God.

In my first year after leaving the hospital for office nursing, the lunchroom conversation with the medical personnel and front office staff turned to Christianity. After a few minutes, one of the staff turned to me and asked, "Are you a Christian?" It was a simple question and I had a simple answer: "Yes!" No explanation seemed to be necessary. All eyes turned to me when a co-worker carefully asked, "But you aren't one of those born-again Christians are you?" The question had a slight sound of disapproval that hung in the air.

The next seconds seemed long to me, creating a moment that stands out in memory. It was a pivotal moment of knowing a firm, "Yes, I am!" response might elicit more scorn than admiration. I knew it would hold me to a higher level of accountability for words and actions. In that moment, I wondered if my life in the workplace appeared more in line with the prevailing worldview than the biblical worldview, causing the need for me to add, "Cross my heart and hope to die!" to be believed. Into that silence I answered quietly but firmly, "Yes, I am!"

This memorable moment raised significant questions for me about my degree of surrender to the lordship of Jesus Christ in every aspect of my life and in every quadrant of my heart. Questions arose as my mind repeatedly returned to that lunchroom scene. Had I compartmentalized my life as a Christian? Was I less surrendered in my nursing work than in my home life? Was I less surrendered in my home life than in my church life? Was I less surrendered in my social life than in my personal life? Could it be that not being fully surrendered in any one part could mean not being truly surrendered in the whole? Into the midst of these questions came the words of David's prayer in Psalm 86.

Teach me your way, LORD, that I may rely on your faithfulness; give me an undivided heart, that I may fear your name. I will praise you, Lord my God, with all my heart; I will glorify your name forever. For great is your love toward me; you have delivered me from the depths, from the realm of the dead.
(PSALM 86:11–13)

God showed me that hearts are meant to be undivided and meant to be wholeheartedly surrendered to His lordship. Even the man who was said to be a man after God's own heart wrestled with having an undivided heart. David's prayer became my prayer. I wanted my heart to be undivided. Going forward, I wanted my life to be unquestionably, recognizably surrendered to God.

This Psalm 86 text gave me three steps for having an undivided heart. First, God is our teacher. Time spent in God's Word reveals to us His truth, His faithfulness, on which we can rely as we trust Him to give us an undivided heart for Him. Next, worship that is pure, praise filled, and glorifying to the name of God opens up every quadrant of our heart to be fully surrendered to Him. And last, the attitude of thankfulness for God's great love, mercy, and salvation keeps our hearts from redividing.

SPIRITUAL HEART SURGERY

Ezekiel provides a second image of an undivided heart:

I will give them an undivided heart and put a new spirit in them; I will remove from them their heart of stone and give them a heart of flesh. Then they will follow my decrees and be careful to keep my laws. They will be my people, and I will be their God."
(EZEKIEL 11:19–20)

God spoke through the prophet Ezekiel to the remnant of His people regarding their future regathering from exile back to their homeland, Israel.

In these Scriptures, God presented the beautiful word picture of the spiritual heart surgery He would perform on His chosen people in their return to Jerusalem one day. This heart procedure was not just for God's people then; it is for us today. God cleanses us in preparation for His spiritual heart surgery when, like David, we seek God's forgiveness for sin that divides our hearts. David prayed, "Cleanse me with hyssop, and I will be clean; wash me, and I will be whiter than snow" (Psalm 51:7).

David repented of the sin that divided his heart between the lure and lusts of the world and obedience to God. The Israelites needed to repent of their sins that divided their hearts between pagan worship and a desire to be saved from pagan nations by Jehovah God. We too must repent of sins that divide our hearts. Only then will we be cleansed and ready for God to replace the sin-hardened divisions of our hearts with new tender heart flesh, to give us an undivided heart in which His Spirit can live, moving us to live fully surrendered to Him.

HEROES OF FAITH

The risk of our hearts becoming divided is ever present, as Satan would love to divide and conquer our hearts, often through adverse circumstances. The story of Joseph in Genesis 37 and 39–50 is a story of life lived for God despite many adversities. Joseph was betrayed by family as he was abandoned and sold into slavery, punished for doing the right thing when faced with sexual temptation, imprisoned for long periods in a foreign land, and forgotten by those he had helped. Through it all, Joseph maintained an undivided faithful heart for His faithful God.

Saint Patrick of Ireland, whose life is celebrated each March by the wearing of green and decorating with shamrocks, was a man like Joseph with an undivided heart for God. Captured by pirates at age 16, he was sold into slavery to a cruel Druid chieftain in Ireland, a wholly heathen nation in the fifth century. During long hours shepherding, Patrick remembered his mother's teachings about Jesus and the words of God she taught him. The adverse circumstances of being enslaved and the truth of God's Word caused Patrick to come to faith in Christ while still a slave. Patrick's confession of faith is found in the Book of Armagh, the Canon of Patrick:

It was there that the Lord opened up my awareness of my lack of faith. Even though it came about late, I recognized my failings. So I turned with all my heart to the Lord my God, and he looked down on my lowliness and had mercy on my youthful ignorance. He guarded me before I knew him, and before I came to wisdom and could distinguish between good and evil. He protected me and consoled me as a father does for his son. That is why I cannot be silent—nor would it be good to do so—about such great blessings and such a gift that the Lord so kindly bestowed in the land of my captivity. This is how we can repay such blessings, when our lives change and we come to know God, to praise and bear witness to his great wonders before every nation under heaven.

Six years passed before Patrick escaped Ireland and returned to Britain. But because the Spirit of God gave him a burden for the heathen in Ireland, he returned to the land of his captivity and, in their language, which he learned while a slave, he preached the gospel of Jesus, baptizing tens of thousands who came to faith in Christ.

UNDIVIDED HEART FOR THAILAND

Missionary biographies like that of Patrick's captured my heart long ago in my early years in missions education. I have learned much about having a fully surrendered heart for God from visiting the lives of missionaries in their biographies. On my bookshelves are *Go Home and Tell*, the story of missionary Bertha Smith in China; *Edwin Dozier of Japan: Man of the Way*, the story of another missionary; *Clothed in White*, the story of Mavis Pate in Gaza; and, most recently added, *A Thousand Times Yes*, the story of missionary doctors Giles and Wana Ann Fort in Zimbabwe, Africa. Each of these is the story of how God used those who had an undivided heart for Him.

We easily recognize wholehearted surrender to Jesus in the lives of missionaries as we listen to their stories and see their tears of joy, as we hear about unreached people of the nations coming to faith in Jesus Christ. We see their surrender, and we admire their giving up what might have been for them here at home to embrace the challenges in the places where they serve. However, if you ask them if they ever think about what their life could have been serving the Lord here and with the resources a lucrative income might have provided, their faces usually become a bit blank, as if this question is irrelevant. I believe the surrendered, undivided heart neither looks back nor regrets. In fact, it sees the joy and satisfaction of missions as priceless.

Doug and Cheryl Derbyshire have surrendered, undivided hearts for God in Thailand. Here is part of their story, with Doug sharing first:

In May 2013, my wife and I went with my team of Thai believers and a small group of students from California Baptist University to Huay

Gae—a small village with a few thousand people not too far south of us. The village was the heart of an area once called "the thieves' forest." There were no believers there. By the end of our day with them, two women prayed to receive Christ, and then a week later, Tem, an 81-year-old woman put her faith in Christ as well.

We began to meet with them and teach them more of the God that they had placed their faith in. Immediately they began to voice their desire to see their neighbors and family come to saving faith in Christ as well. Soon, Tem's 41-year-old son gave his life to the Lord as well. The following week, we met all together for worship. The brand-new believers from Huay Gae joined together with our team from Bangkla, and together we praised and worshipped the Lord. By all evidences, it was the first time that believers had gathered in Huay Gae to worship God since the dawn of creation.

On that day, I thought to myself, This is the joy that is mine, and the driving force that compels me to continue this work that the Lord has given to me—to see people reconciled to God and then gather to worship Him in places where He had never been praised since the world was created.

A month later, we went with another group of volunteers from Arizona, along with a small contingent of Thai believers up into the mountains of northern Thailand. We traveled more than 12 hours by van, then 2 more hours by four-wheel-drive vehicle up winding roads and rock-strewn paths to a small isolated tribal village. We treated the sick until it was too late to return—the road wasn't safe at night. So we spent the night on the mountain. After setting up the tents, our group gathered together for a night of worship and praise. I spoke on Hosea 1 and God's heart to call those who are not His people to Himself that they might become His people and obtain His mercy. Then we shared testimonies and sang songs of worship and praise.

One of the believers who came with us was from the same tribe as the people of the village. He closed our time together by thanking everyone for sharing his burden to see his people saved. He said that he was so glad that the Lord had allowed us to share the gospel with the village. He said, "This is a wonderful day. Not only were we able to share Christ with people who did not know Him, but tonight we praised God together on this mountain. It is the first time that God has been praised on this mountain since the beginning of time." It was inspiring to hear him speak—and it amazed me to hear him voice the same heart that I had when seeing God praised in Huay Gae for the first time.

Doug wrote more about the joy his work brought him:

This is my work and my joy, and it is a mighty joy: seeing people made God's people, and seeing God worshipped where He had never received His due worship before. I have left America and the familiar to serve my Lord here. How could I have a moment's regret? Paul says, "I have made it my aim to preach, and to preach where Christ has not been named . . . so that those who have not heard shall understand" [see Romans 15:20–21 NKJV]. This was Paul's work and his joy, and it is mine.

Cheryl added her comments, revealing her undivided heart:

Over the 20-plus years that Doug and I have been on the missions field, God has given us these kinds of opportunities time and time again. Often when we are in the States, people make comments about how impressed they are about the sacrifice we have made to give our lives to such a work when we could be in the States, still doing God's work, but with Doug bringing home a doctor's salary. My thought is often, *There is no sacrifice here.* The value of worshipping on a mountain where God had never been worshipped is priceless.

APPLICATION

❧ Spend time in prayer, examining with God your heart of surrender. Ask God to identify any areas of hardness that have formed to keep you from full surrender to the lordship of Jesus Christ.

❧ What lessons for living in wholehearted surrender do you learn from the undivided hearts of Joseph, Patrick of Ireland, and Doug and Cheryl Derbyshire?

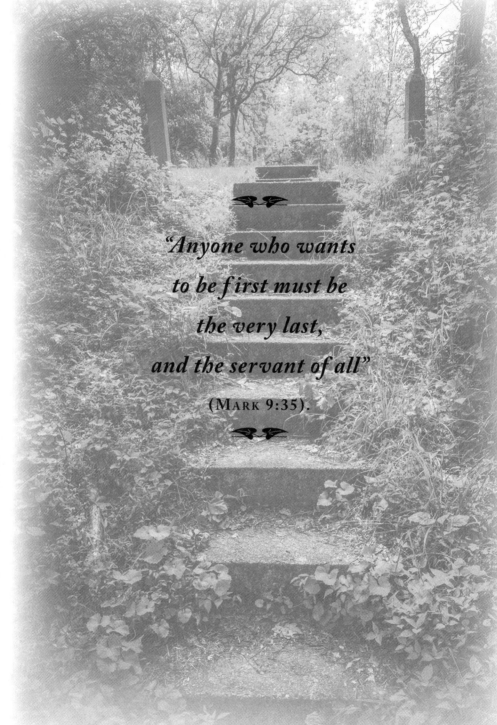

"Anyone who wants

to be first must be

the very last,

and the servant of all"

(MARK 9:35).

CHAPTER 11

Wholehearted Sacrifice

O FTEN WE LEARN AS MUCH from the lives of those who struggled and fled from God's call as we learn from the fully surrendered lives of those who took up their cross to live for God sacrificially for God.

Jesus, after sharing about His impending suffering and death, raised the bar for what it meant to be His follower:

"Whoever wants to be my disciple must deny themselves and take up their cross and follow me. For whoever wants to save their life will lose it, but whoever loses their life for me and for the gospel will save it."
(MARK 8:34–35)

No more would the literal following of this Rabbi Jesus on dusty roads lead to peaceful gardens and pastoral hillsides where His lessons of God's love would be taught. Nor would the prophesied arrival of Messiah be proclaimed as a time for triumphant restoration of the kingdom of Israel to glory and productivity. Instead, Messiah's coming would be equated forevermore with the sacrifice of Jesus' life so we might have eternal life. Disciples of Jesus would now be expected to surrender wholeheartedly to Him, to be willing to lose their lives in His life, and to take up the cross of following the Lord wherever He led.

The Gospel writer Mark would have understood these expectations of which Jesus spoke as he chronicled the events of Jesus' ministry. Many theologians believe that in Mark 14, the author was writing from his own experience in the garden of Gethsemane because one incident at the arrest of Jesus appears only in his Gospel: "A young man, wearing nothing but a linen garment, was following Jesus. When they seized him, he fled naked, leaving his garment behind" (Mark 14:51–52). Although this young unnamed man did not flee the garden alone (all who were with Jesus that night deserted Him), he was probably the youngest in the group and more agile than former tax collectors or fishermen. He was most likely the fastest, wriggling away from the soldiers so recklessly that those with a grip on him had only his clothing left in their hands.

If this young man was Mark, imagine the pain he must have experienced, having deserted Jesus, the One who had drawn him in, shown him love, and then laid down His life for the young man's own sins the very next day. Imagine Mark's sorrow, revisiting the memory of his fleeing-the-scene-of-the-crime experience as he heard the stories of Jesus and the Passion of Jesus retold day after day, town after town, by the disciples.

Young Mark, or John Mark as the Bible often refers to him, required much patience and nurturing along the way. A second flight scene marked his life when he suddenly, and apparently without permission, left Paul and Barnabas in Perga in the midst of a missions journey (Acts 13:13). Many have conjectured on why John Mark left. I wonder if his heart was unable to bear the degree of sacrifice required for the journey, if it could not persevere under the daily cross carrying of persecution and potential for arrest or even losing his own life.

FLIGHT OF AN UNCROSSED HEART

Mark's story of flight reminds us of Jonah, who stands out as a very poor biblical model of a missionary. Although Jonah is most associated with a big fish event and whining over a withering vine, the author of 2 Kings described Jonah as a servant of God and a prophet. God used Jonah to prophesy that the border of Israel from Hamath in Syria south to the Dead Sea would be restored. King Jeroboam II accomplished this in 793 BC (2 Kings 14:25). Some eight years later, according to some schools of thought, God again called on Jonah; this time the assignment was to bring His message to Nineveh (Jonah 1).

We may wonder, *Why did Jonah, in only his second recorded assignment from God, not only refuse to go but actually flee from God?* His first assignment turned out well with the prophecy fulfilled. So, why? Familiarity with this part of Jonah's life—running from God, spending three days in the belly of a big fish, getting a second chance, and then complaining about the results of the mission—perhaps, makes it easy for us to think negatively toward Jonah. From our church pew or comfortable place of Bible reading, we might even condemn his flight as well as his prejudice against Nineveh.

We could compare this prophet's assignment to go to the great city of Nineveh in the evil empire of Assyria with an assignment today to go to a hotbed of the world's worst places of despotism and cruel practices towards others. This might be like God saying to you or me, *Go to the great city of Pyongyang or Kabul or Tripoli and preach against it, because its wickedness has come before me.* Assyria was considered the fiercest of Israel's enemy nations.

According to Bible History Online:

Their very name became a byword for cruelty and atrocity. They skinned their prisoners alive, and cut off various body parts to inspire terror in their enemies. There [are] records of Assyrian officials pulling out tongues and displaying mounds of human skulls all to bring about stark horror and wealthy tribute from surrounding nations. Nowhere are the pages of history more bloody than in the records of their wars.

This helps us understand why Jonah wanted to run more than he wanted to please God.

Would we question what purpose a call from God to go to these cities would serve and run the other way? Would we, too, panic and flee because of fear? Would we, out of prejudice, lay down the cross Jesus has asked us to take up to be His disciple? Serving at God's bidding requires sacrificing our own purposes, fears, and prejudices. Like for Jonah, the act of fleeing from the call of God starts today's disciple of Jesus on a stormy journey, which may result in serious consequences that get that disciple's attention.

Jonah 1 reminds us that when we run in the opposite direction of God's call, we run with "uncrossed," unwilling-to-sacrifice hearts, hearts that have not taken up their cross to follow Jesus. We think by running, we might save our life, not lose it; however, in the running, God reveals His truths and consequences. The powerful storm in Jonah's flight revealed God as both Creator and Ruler of all, nature and mankind— yes, even Jonah. The plight of the innocent sailors revealed Jonah's guilt of disobedience to God's command. The push overboard revealed how his life could have been the sacrifice for the sailors instead of being a willing sacrifice to serve God wholeheartedly.

ULTIMATE SACRIFICE

Fox's Book of Martyrs is a difficult read for any Christian. It presents, in detail, the terrible means the world has used to attempt to stop the gospel of Jesus from being preached. Of the 12 apostles, all but John died martyrs' deaths, although John was thrown into a cauldron of boiling oil from which he miraculously emerged uninjured, and then was banished to the isle of Patmos. James the Great was beheaded. Philip was scourged and crucified. Matthew was slain with a halberd, a weapon with ax blade, pick, and spear. James the Lesser was beaten, stoned, and had his brains dashed out with a fuller's club. Matthias, who replaced Judas, was stoned and beheaded. Andrew was crucified on a cross. Bartholomew was beaten and crucified. Peter, Thaddaeus, and Simon were crucified. And Thomas was thrust through by a spear.

These were the threats to first-century Christians who preached the gospel of Jesus. Threats against those who obey the Great Commission of Jesus to carry the gospel into all the world have continued for nearly 2,000 years and are as real today for twenty-first-century disciples as they were then.

Consider the words of Dietrich Bonhoeffer from his book, *The Cost of Discipleship*, "When Christ calls a man, He bids him come and die." Bonhoeffer left the safety of the United States and returned to World War II Germany saying,

"I have come to the conclusion that I made a mistake in coming to America. . . . I shall have no right to participate in the reconstruction of Christian life in Germany after the war if I do not share the trials of this time with my people."

Bonhoeffer was ultimately arrested and executed for his part in rescuing German Jews and his other efforts in active resistance against the Nazi regime in Germany.

Jim Elliot, martyred deep in the jungle of Ecuador, wrote these words in his journal: "He is no fool who gives what he cannot keep to gain what he cannot lose." Elliot sacrificed his life for Christ long before the first Auca spear penetrated his body in 1956. He sacrificed his life for Christ when he left the safety of home to take the gospel of Jesus to unreached Auca Indians in Ecuador.

The life of Dr. Martha Myers was also sacrificed much earlier than the day she was gunned down by terrorists, martyred for the sake of the gospel at Jibla Baptist Hospital in Yemen. Barbara Joiner, in her book *The Story of Martha Myers,* recounts words of Bill O'Brien, former vice-president of the Foreign Mission Board (now International Mission Board), shared in a memorial service for Martha Myers at Samford University:

Dr. Martha's life was not taken. She had long since given it away. It started at First Baptist Church of Avondale, Georgia, where she made her profession of faith. You could call it "a long obedience in the same direction" [referencing Eugene H. Peterson's *A Long Obedience in the Same Direction*]. Her life was centered in the person of Jesus Christ. With an undivided heart, she gave herself to the Yemeni people.

These are the life-and-death stories of hearts crossed with the truth of Jesus, hearts surrendered to Jesus, hearts undivided for Jesus, and hearts sacrificed wholeheartedly in the name of Jesus. How do these examples fit with our everyday relatively safe lives? Are we ever called on to lay down our lives?

REAL QUESTIONS FOR REAL LIFE

Many years ago, a young woman moved to our area and joined our church. She was married to a man who did not love the Lord, a man far from saving faith. She loved him dearly, and prayers for his salvation dominated her prayer life. Our church faithfully prayed for her husband. One summer weekend, she and her husband and their little boy were invited to go camping with neighbors, a Christian couple with whom they had become friends. The day before embarking on the camping trip, her husband was called in to work the weekend. He urged her to go and enjoy the time away with friends.

One night, after settling her little boy down in their tent and being sure he was asleep, she went to the other couple's tent for a time of devotion and prayer. When morning came, the little boy was found wandering in the campground, saying his mommy wouldn't wake up. She and her friends were victims of carbon monoxide poisoning from a kerosene lantern. The news was devastating and rocked her family's world and our church family's. Ministry began to her husband and little boy: meals, transportation to preschool, and babysitting. The grieving young man found comfort in his wife's friends.

One Sunday, many months later, on entering the church sanctuary, I noted a palpable "something" in the atmosphere. I was keenly aware of this for several minutes as people entered and filled the pews. And then I watched as the slumped shoulders of the widower came in and took a seat. What I had sensed was the Spirit of God filling the sanctuary in preparation for this man to arrive. At the end of the service when the pastor gave an invitation, our friend's husband tearfully made his way to the front and gave his life to Jesus. What rejoicing took place that day! What a balm this was to the sadness of losing a friend.

That morning as the new salvation experience unfolded, a young woman whose husband was not a believer was sitting with her daughter. Later she shared with others her daughter's question on the way home from church: "Mom, do mothers have to die for fathers to be saved?" The mother grappled with the best answer for that poignant question and finally responded, "No, because Jesus has already given His life for the father's salvation." She explained that terrible accidents sometimes happen, but God doesn't cause them. She told her little girl that God wanted something wonderful to be the result of this tragedy and now, praise God, it was.

This true story caused me to ponder my degree of willingness to give my life for the spiritually lost lives of some of my friends and relatives. Questions seemed to come to me from God: *But what about you? Are you willing to die if the outcome means their salvation and eternal life?* These are real questions for real life.

APPLICATION

❧ Think back to a personal experience of running like Jonah from God's call to you to sacrifice your life purposes, personal fears, and private prejudices in serving. What were the consequences and what was the outcome?

❧ In light of the ultimate sacrifices of martyrs and the glorious result of a young woman's death, how willingly will you take up your cross, even if it should mean losing your life for Christ and for the sake of the gospel?

"What good is it
for someone to gain
the whole world,
yet forfeit their soul?"

(M<small>ARK</small> 8:36)

CHAPTER 12

All-for-You Sacrifice

*I*N OUR ALL-ABOUT-ME WORLD, Jesus' self-sacrificing life is the antithesis of man's desire for self-determination. In our all-about-me world, Jesus' life is the authentic model for man to live an all-for-You sacrificial life.

Self-determination has been innate in men and women since the first bites of the prohibited fruit in the Garden of Eden. It has misdirected mankind, causing towers like Babel to be built, golden calves to be worshipped, adulterous relationships to be rationalized, man's laws to supersede God's law, and 30 pieces of silver to buy betrayal. Used over and over again, self-determination continues to be one of Satan's tools to deter anyone who would respond to Jesus' invitation to be His disciple. Self-determination is the biggest deterrent to self-sacrifice.

Random House Kernerman Webster's College Dictionary defines *self-determination* as "freedom to live as one chooses, or to act or decide without consulting others; freedom of a people to determine the way in which they shall be governed and whether or not they shall be self-governed."

We see daily the freedom of self-determination in media, government, business, and even religion. Even in the poorest strata of society, self-determination can still be found. Among the homeless living in the secluded woods of my city, the drive for self-determination is apparent as these men and women choose the rigors of living rough over the warmth and safety of shelters that have necessary rules. Even in the early years of life, self-determination can be noted. From the church's nursery on Sunday mornings, we can hear self-determination among the toddlers as a little mouth spits out its pacifier and cries, "No! Mine!" Even within the church, evidence of overriding self-determination is strong. The rising incidence of church splits, failed marriages, and personal bankruptcy points to self-determination.

WE WANT MORE

A recent commercial gives us a glimpse of this innate drive for self-determination. A man is sitting with three preschoolers and asks, "Who thinks more is better than less?" One little girl says, "More is better than less because if stuff is not less . . . if there's more less stuff then you might, might want to have some more, and your parents just don't let you because there's only a little." It is cute how she runs on a bit aimlessly. But then she adds, "We want more. We want more. Like, you really like it. You want more." This wanting more is a huge piece of the self-determination inherent in man. We see it in the preschooler who may not share. We see it in the overstuffed shopping bags lugged along our malls by the buyers. We see it in the acres of storage units where we store our stuff, there being no more room in our spacious homes. And we see it in the maxed-out credit cards and depleted cash reserves of families and businesses.

The Gospel writer Mark tells us that Jesus' words *"Whoever wants to be my disciple"* (8:34) were given not only to the Twelve traveling with Him but also to the crowds who followed Him, listening to His teachings and watching for His miracles. On that day, Jesus marked discipleship with the elements of surrender and sacrifice, of setting aside self-determination to become a living sacrifice:

Then he called the crowd to him along with his disciples and said: "Whoever wants to be my disciple must deny themselves and take up their cross and follow me. For whoever wants to save their life will lose it, but whoever loses their life for me and for the gospel will save it. What good is it for someone to gain the whole world, yet forfeit their soul? Or what can anyone give in exchange for their soul?"
(MARK 8:34–37)

Calling the crowd to join his disciples, he said, "Anyone who intends to come with me has to let me lead. You're not in the driver's seat; I am. Don't run from suffering; embrace it. Follow me and I'll show you how. Self-help is no help at all. Self-sacrifice is the way, my way, to saving yourself, your true self. What good would it do to get everything you want and lose you, the real you? What could you ever trade your soul for?"
(MARK 8:34–37 THE MESSAGE)

The Message presents these verses with Jesus' passion for people to become His followers not only in name, but also in word and deed.

Jesus could teach about surrender because in becoming the Son of man, the incarnate Christ, He had submitted to the will of His Father God. He could teach about sacrifice because He was born on earth to die for the people of this earth. His duty, though, was not just to be born and to die; His duty was first to be the perfect example for us through His life and then the perfect sacrifice for us through His death.

GLORIA'S STORY

Gloria came to a time in her life when self-determination for stress-free retirement living would come up against sacrificing that lifestyle to obey a call from God to shoulder a new responsibility in missions. The following is her story:

As a GA and YWA [member] (Girls' Auxiliary and Young Woman's Auxiliary), I listened to missionaries share their experiences and hoped one day I would go on a missions trip. Years later, after hearing a couple share about their missions trip abroad, I whispered to my husband [Bill], "Wouldn't it be great if we could go on a missions trip after we retire?"

Five years into retirement, my husband and I were invited to participate in a weeklong Missions Vision Tour for churches with the Appalachian Regional Ministries. We agreed to go, my husband saying he would tag along as my bodyguard. Even before the trip began, I was asked if I would lead a missions trip after we returned. I quickly responded, "Oh! No! I can't lead a trip, but I'll go as a team member." I did not feel qualified to be a missions team leader; but more than that, I did not want to shoulder the responsibilities, feel the pressures of leadership, or give the time required to a new missions initiative! Resolved to simply observe and report back to our church, we joined the tour group.

The tour took us through three states where we met directors of missions and heard about the need for short-term volunteers from NAMB missionaries serving the people of Appalachia. When we arrived in Lynch, Kentucky, a former coal-mining town nestled in the Appalachian Mountains, my heart was crushed by all the poverty I saw. Meeting at the former high school gymnasium, we heard the testimonies of missionaries Lonnie and Belinda Riley. As their stories wove their way into my heart and soul, God convicted me then and there. I knew I would return to Lynch as team member or even as the leader. Words I had recently read came to my mind: "Will you go where you don't know and never be the same?" When my husband heard about the construction opportunities for volunteers, he, too, got excited and his hand flew across the notepad taking notes. He wanted to return to Lynch, Kentucky, as well.

Words were bubbling out of my mouth the next week when I attempted to describe my feelings to my friend Debby. She could hear the enthusiasm in my voice, see the excitement in my eyes, and feel the love I had for the folks of Lynch. When our missions pastor moved, all eyes turned to Bill and me to lead the first missions team to Kentucky. Where previously I had stated an emphatic "No!" now I was ready to sacrifice my responsibility-free days to take up the cross of leading the missions team with my husband by my side as coleader. We were blessed to lead teams to Lynch, Kentucky, for seven years on mission for our God.

The sum total of Jesus' earthly life and death is His all-for-You living for His Father God and the highest level of self-sacrifice in history. In His last moment of life, Jesus said, "It is finished" (John 19:30). His purposes on earth were complete; He had led the perfect life, made the perfect sacrifice, and left the perfect example to follow. As followers of Jesus, we are called to follow His example by carrying the cross of sacrificial living. How do we do this? How do we set self-determination aside to follow Christ in living-sacrifice mode? How do we find the joy of self-sacrifice, as did Gloria and Bill?

FOUR PRINCIPLES FOR SACRIFICIAL LIVING

Paul's letters provide four principles of sacrificial living, beginning in Romans:

Therefore, I urge you, brothers and sisters, in view of God's mercy, to offer your bodies as a living sacrifice, holy and pleasing to God—this is your true and proper worship. Do not conform to the pattern of this world, but be transformed by the renewing of your mind. Then you will be able to test and approve what God's will is—his good, pleasing and perfect will. (ROMANS 12:1–2)

First, renew your mind! Paul urges nonconformity saying, "Do not conform to the pattern of this world, but be transformed by the renewing of your mind" (v. 2). We considered the biblical world-view through the life of Jesus in chapter 9, "Upright Living in an Upside-Down World." In this chapter we noted how the drive for self-determination undermines the becoming a disciple of Jesus. Worldview and self-determination are activities of the mind. To the Shema's command to love the Lord our God with all our heart, soul, and strength, Jesus added the word *mind* (Mark 12:30). He knew that our minds were so easily undermined that unless we loved God with all of our minds, we would never give up the freedom of self-determination, never turn over the controls and invite Jesus to take the driver's seat as Mark described (8:34).

The story of the rich young ruler in Luke 18:18–24 is an example. This wealthy young man had disciplined himself to keep all the rules of the Jewish faith, yet in his mind, he had no assurance of eternal life. He sought Jesus with the hope in his heart that this good teacher would tell him what to do. But when called to sacrifice all his possessions, all the wealth that would forever define him as the rich young ruler, and when invited to join the disciples that had left their nets and all behind, he could not wrap his mind around total sacrifice and left sad. Choosing to be a living sacrifice that lays everything at the feet of Jesus and our lives on His altar comes from loving the Lord, not just with all our hearts but also with all our minds.

Second, keep your mind spiritually protected.

Put on the full armor of God,
so that you can take your stand against the devil's schemes.
Take the helmet of salvation and the sword of the Spirit,
which is the word of God.
(EPHESIANS 6:11, 17)

Paul used the analogy of something familiar to his readers—armor worn by Roman soldiers—to delineate the ways Christians must arm themselves, not for physical battle, but for spiritual battle. We know the importance of helmets to protect the brain from injury in contact sports, biking, and skateboarding. The helmet of salvation (v. 17) protects our minds from being injured by the devil's schemes. The devil is proficient at planting doubts in our minds about salvation. He wants us to think we have so much past sin and shame that we can never be truly forgiven, never be good enough for God. The devil points to the problems of life and tempts us to think that if we were really forgiven, God would not allow difficulties in our lives. We find confidence in our salvation and eternal life with Father God through faith in the Lord Jesus; we wear the helmet of salvation to protect our minds, to protect that confidence; and that confidence strengthens our desire to be a living sacrifice for God.

Third, do everything you do in the name of the Lord Jesus.

And whatever you do, whether in word or deed,
do it all in the name of the Lord Jesus,
giving thanks to God the Father through him.
(COLOSSIANS 3:17)

With the all-inclusive word *whatever,* Paul shows us that everything we do must be measured against God's call to live fully for Him. Paul wrote, "Whatever you do, whether in word or deed." All our words, all our conversations, and all our thoughts; all our goals, all our plans, and all our actions—all these are included in Paul's *whatever.* "Do it all in the name of the Lord Jesus." In today's vernacular, this concept is captured in the word *totally!* Do it totally in the name of the Lord Jesus. Being a living sacrifice is giving up saying what we cannot say in the same breath as the precious name of our Lord Jesus; it is giving up doing what we cannot do as a named follower of Jesus. The verse ends with "giving thanks to God the Father through him." Paul reminds us that being a living sacrifice is a privilege for which we are to give God thanks.

Fourth and last, value the knowing of Christ Jesus, counting all else worthless by comparison.

But whatever were gains to me I now consider loss for the sake of Christ. What is more, I consider everything a loss because of the surpassing worth of knowing Christ Jesus my Lord, for whose sake I have lost all things. I consider them garbage, that I may gain Christ.
(PHILIPPIANS 3:7–8)

Paul admonishes us with this *whatever* (v. 7) to count everything we have been and everything we have held dear as loss, just in case we have any shred of holding back from sacrificial living with thoughts we are exempted by some religious pedigree. No religious pedigree, no worldly status, no financial standing can compare with the supreme value of knowing Christ Jesus; all else is rubbish.

Some disciples are called to give the ultimate sacrifice, laying down their lives, in taking up the cross to follow Jesus. Some disciples are called to live sacrificially in hard places, lonely places, dark places to share the gospel with the lost. But all who would be Jesus' disciple are called to be ready and willing to sacrifice time, relationships, resources, and privileges to take up the cross and answer His call; all are to be living sacrifices. Watchman Nee wrote, "For God no cost is too high. Anything can be sacrificed if only we may please Him. Let us daily learn to be obedient children." The life of Watchman Nee, a twentieth-century Chinese Christian church leader and author who was persecuted by the Communist regime and imprisoned for his faith, painted a picture of all-for-You sacrifice.

APPLICATION

❧ How has self-determination conflicted with God's call to you to be a living sacrifice for Him?

❧ In what place of service is God calling you to present yourself anew in sacrifice?

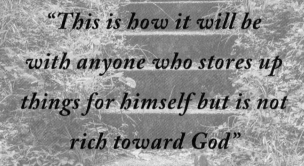

"This is how it will be with anyone who stores up things for himself but is not rich toward God"

(LUKE 12:21).

CHAPTER 13

Heart of Gold

❧❧

ANYTHING CAN BE SACRIFICED if only we may please Him." These, again, are the words of Watchman Nee, the twentieth-century Chinese Christian church leader and author persecuted by the Communist regime and imprisoned for his faith until his death in 1972. His words and his life direct us further into our look at sacrificial living. If surrender must be wholehearted to be pleasing to God, then sacrificial living must also be wholehearted in order to be fully pleasing to God. Is there some line demarking where a surrendered life becomes a living sacrifice? If so, perhaps the only place we could distinguish a line would be in a look beneath the surface at the spiritual heart.

Jesus spoke often of the heart, the important matters of the heart, as recorded in the Gospels. Jesus spoke of the heart as a place for purity, treasure, humility, forgiveness, and, finally, love for God and neighbor. Jesus also spoke of the heart as a place where sin works to replace these beautiful qualities; it works to replace them with callousness, doubts, selfishness, and evil desires. Jesus summed up His teaching on the heart with these words: "For where your treasure is, there your heart will be also" (Luke 12:34). Jesus knew that if the treasure of a man's or a woman's heart was family, then that person would do everything possible to bless his or her family regardless of personal sacrifice. He knew if the treasure was success with accompanying wealth and prestige, then that person would sacrifice anything to reach that personal pinnacle. But if the treasure was Jesus, then they would sacrifice all out of love for Him.

Do you remember from the previous chapter the sadness of the rich young ruler who walked away from Jesus, walked away from sacrificing whatever it took to be a follower of Jesus (Luke 18:18–24)? Before that incident, Jesus presented to a crowd of many thousands a parable about a rich fool who treasured the abundance of his stored up bumper crops over the needs of others (Luke 12:16–21). Jesus told of that rich man's woeful end and finished His parable with a convicting statement: "This is how it will be with anyone who stores up things for himself but is not rich toward God" (v. 21). I wonder if the young ruler had been among those thousands and heard that parable but had not let Jesus' words sink into his riches-loving heart, his self-treasuring heart.

Watchman Nee, in his book *Love Not the World,* wrote of the importance of attitude of the heart in sacrifice:

You and I must be perfectly willing to part with anything at any moment. It matters not whether I leave two thousand dollars or merely two. What matters is whether I can leave what ever I have without a twinge of regret.

MELISSA'S AND FITZ'S HEARTS FOR MISSIONS

Melissa and John "Fitz" Fitzwater were willing to part from their comfortable and familiar life in North Carolina, to leave all they had without a twinge of regret, for the rigors of missions life in Lynch, Kentucky, as North American Mission Board (NAMB)–appointed, Mission Service Corps–funded missionaries. Here is their story from Melissa's point of view:

We make choices daily: what to eat, what to wear, what to do, where to go, how to behave. A very poor choice I made was to put God on a shelf for more than a decade. The best choice I made was to come back to the way of the Cross and follow *Him*. It was this best choice that began my journey that led me to my husband, to become a mom, to be a leader of women in our church, and to develop a heart for missions.

As a child growing up, we were taught about missions and prayed for missionaries in our own country and in countries throughout the world. I remember praying for a lady who left New England to ride on horse or donkey to teach people about Jesus in the mountains of Kentucky. As a child I thought, *Who wouldn't want to spend their life riding a horse?*

In the 1990s, I made several trips to Mexico with our church's missions team. A passion for missions grew and brought back childhood memories of missionary stories.

Fast-forward to 2005. My sister was preparing to go on a missions trip to a place called Lynch, Kentucky (sounded like a foreign land to me!). Her church invited me to join the team. How exciting it was to go "on mission" for the first time with my sister!

The following year, 2006, I was again invited to be a part of the Kentucky missions team. While preparing for Kentucky, my husband was preparing for his first missions trip, a missions trip to Cambodia. His prayer was, "Lord, change me." That is exactly what God would do.

On my second day in Kentucky, the Lord gave me the verse Proverbs 16:9 (NASB): "The mind of man plans his way, but the LORD directs his steps." While Fitz was praying, "Lord, change me," the Father had me praying, "Be ready." Fitz came home from Cambodia and was informed he no longer had a job.

Twelve months later, Fitz, still unemployed and with no excuse for not going with me, joined the missions team to Lynch, Kentucky. We watched the Father's work in our lives that week in late October of 2007 until we knew with certainty we were to serve the Lord wholeheartedly in Lynch, Kentucky. In choosing to be a follower of Christ in missions, we had to leave our home, our children (18 and 20), and a little grandson. We had to deny the only life we knew and take up the cross the Father was giving us, a cross of burden for the lost souls of southeastern Kentucky.

"To this you were called, because Christ suffered for you, leaving you an example, that you should follow in his steps" (1 Peter 2:21). Fitz and

I have been called to serve the Father in the mountains of southeastern Kentucky. Jesus was and is our example, and we are doing our best to follow in His steps. Just like the missionary I prayed for as a child, we are doing all we can to teach the people in the mountains of Kentucky about Jesus. And, as the Lord would have it, Miss Alice Swanson, that missionary I mentioned, served here in Harlan County, as we do today!

❦

Melissa is my sister. It has been my joy to see God redeem, restore, and relocate her and her husband to Lynch, Kentucky. The treasure of their heart now is the joy of giving their all for the gospel to be proclaimed.

HEART INTEGRITY

King David's sacrificial giving to the building of God's temple is recorded in 1 Chronicles 29. David gave of his personal resources, silver and gold and jewels, setting a high standard for giving and a challenge to the people for personal sacrificial giving. David declared through praise and prayer that all we have is from God and still belongs to God. Since his heart had been tested by God on several occasions during his reign as king, he could attest to God's pleasure only in full integrity of the heart.

Our generosity in giving is but a shadow of God's giving to us. We must never forget our God, Jehovah Jireh ("YHWH will provide"), has provided all we have so we can provide for His kingdom work. He has blessed us so we can bless others. Our sacrificial giving is only a shadow of the sacrifice Jesus made for us. Jesus paid it all so that we live redeemed and find joy in living and giving sacrificially.

Several years ago, I took my older GA® members on a five-day missions trip to Lynch, Kentucky, to work with my sister and brother-in-law and other nearby missionaries. The girls prepared for this trip for six months with prayer, planning, and collecting items to be distributed in food and clothing ministries. Each day in Kentucky, the girls enthusiastically interacted with people with great physical and spiritual needs as they distributed food at the Loaves and Fishes Ministry food pantry, sorted clothes, and planted flowers at Freedom Center Ministries, and prayerwalked at Club 180. Each night in our devotional times, the girls reflected on the day's experiences, journaled their thoughts, and prayed for those they had met and with whom they had shared about Jesus. On our last night, I asked the girls to talk about one major thing God had shown them on this missions trip. One of the girls, who was from a comfortable family without financial concerns, told the group she learned God had blessed her with more than enough so she could bless others. That was a major heart step for this young girl towards sacrificial living and giving.

At the end of David's song of praise in 1 Chronicles 29, he asked God a question and then acknowledged Him as the source of blessings: "But who am I, and who are my people, that we should be able to give as generously as this? Everything comes from you, and we have given you only what comes from your hand" (v. 14). Later David declared his heart's intent: "I know, my God, that you test the heart and are pleased with integrity. All these things I have given willingly and with honest intent" (v. 17).

David, as he gave sacrificially from the deep pockets of his personal resources to honor God with the building of the Temple, truly demonstrated a heart of gold-star integrity. If David had read the Book of Job, he would have said with Job, "But he knows the way that I take; when he has tested me, I will come forth as gold" (Job 23:10). David ended his reign as king with integrity and a giving heart of gold.

HEART OF GOLD LEGACIES

David George, a foundation president, has seen the commingling of integrity and hearts of gold in legacies left behind for others and provided some examples:

In 11½ years at the WMU Foundation, I have been privileged to see numerous acts of charity and generosity and have worked with people who are giving so that others can benefit and typically want no recognition. In fact, I have been admonished more than once by generous donors to be exceedingly careful that no one learns their identity.

The stories that come to mind are many and quite varied. The donors are young and old, men and women, and well off and very modest in terms of their financial situation. Charlie Burch, the man whose estate gift was the largest ever in our history (so far), was not well known and even his friends did not know the size of his estate. His simple request "that the money be used to spread the gospel overseas" was based on his trust in WMU; and it continues to amaze me that he expected no recognition or elaborate plans. Just tell the story of Jesus to those who need to hear of His love.

Other examples quickly come to mind: the gifts of children who gather coins, doing extra chores to help provide goats in Croatia or chickens in Liberia; the grandmother in Illinois who rolled dimes to give to missions and taught this to her daughter and granddaughter only days before her death; and the past scholarship recipient who now gives every year to support future scholarship recipients. Some of our largest contributions come from retired missionaries, not because they have the most, but perhaps because they understand missions the best.

The story and sacrificial gift of a retired missionary come to mind as I read the words of Jesus in Mark 8:34: "Whoever wants to be my disciple must deny themselves and take up their cross and follow me." Kate Ellen Gruver attended the WMU Training School and heeded God's call to serve Him in Palestine, where she ran an orphanage for many years. Upon her return to the States, she became the first female professional staff member of the Home Mission Board (now North American Mission Board), specializing in interfaith witness. After retirement, she continued to serve the Lord through WMU and as a Sunday School teacher at Wieuca Road Baptist Church.

Kate Ellen left her entire estate to the Foundation with the stipulation that it be used for scholarships for female students at the Arab Baptist Theological Seminary in Lebanon. Why there? Because it is the only school in the region where Christians can study without persecution. Students come from all over the Middle East to attend this seminary to be trained as pastors, missionaries, Christian counselors, etc. Many of the couples who want to minister together could not attend if their wives did not receive a Kate Ellen Gruver Scholarship.

Another piece of Kate Ellen's story represents her sacrificial giving. She was born in the Panama Canal Zone, where her father worked with General Gorgas to help eradicate yellow fever. For many years, her home was in the Atlanta, Georgia, area, where she worked and retired. But, as she sensed her life on earth was coming to a close, she made a very significant move back to Nashville, Tennessee, where her family home had been and where her family had selected a grave site for her. She moved away from her lifelong friends in order to conserve burial costs, specifically so that more money would be left in her estate to go to missions. Kate Ellen truly is an example of sacrificing one's own short-term personal needs and desires for the long-term good of others.

Charlie Burch and Kate Ellen Gruver had hearts of gold, leaving a legacy to support their heart's treasure, God and His mission.

APPLICATION

❧ What is the treasure of your heart?

❧ Can you think of anything you would even hesitate to deny yourself or give up should God call you to do so?

❧ What level of integrity does God find in your sacrificial giving?

❧ How will your giving move toward the gold standard of King David, Charlie Burch, and Kate Ellen Gruver?

"Many who are first

will end up last,

and the last first"

(Mark 10:29–31).

CHAPTER 14

Two Sides to the Sacrifice Story

❧❧

J UST AS THERE ARE TWO SIDES to every story, there are two sides to the stories of sacrifice for the missionary families in previous chapters. You saw one side as you read the stories of the Brindles, the Millars, the Derbyshires, and the Fitzwaters—although they see no sacrifice in the joy of obediently serving in missions. According to *The Message*, this sacrifice of leaving home and family and land to follow Jesus leads to "the Great Reversal":

❧❧

Jesus said, "Mark my words, no one who sacrifices house, brothers, sisters, mother, father, children, land—whatever—because of me and the

Message will lose out. They'll get it all back, but multiplied many times in homes, brothers, sisters, mothers, children, and land—but also in troubles. And then the bonus of eternal life! This is once again the Great Reversal: Many who are first will end up last, and the last first."
(Mark 10:29–31 *The Message*)

This Scripture shows that the sacrifice of taking up our cross and following Jesus actually results in gain. This is once again upright living in an upside-down world.

However, the other side to the story of sacrifice is that made by parents of missionaries. As their children are commissioned to far-off states and countries, dangerous inner cities, and primitive villages, missionary parents are left behind. Many parents count it a privilege to have their children called by God to career missions and support them faithfully with prayer. Most entrust their children to God's care, holding back their tears and fears as separation approaches. All face the reality of personal sacrifice as their children and grandchildren walk into a missions life far away. This is true as well of those who have left home and family to embrace the call to missions.

NEW UNDERSTANDING OF SACRIFICE

Jim (whose last name is omitted for security reasons) tells the other side of the sacrifice story from a two-sided personal perspective:

I grew up in Texas and attended Baylor University in Waco, then Southwestern Seminary in Fort Worth. All my extended family lived in Texas. All my personal and spiritual experience was in Texas. When my parents heard that I was called to New England to serve as a pastor, they were completely supportive. They had long ago given me to the Lord and wanted me to follow God's call, even though it meant very infrequent visits with their grandchildren and oldest son.

I did not realize what sacrifice they made until our own son, who all through his growing up years said he wanted to be a lawyer, surrendered to God's call to the ministry. We were, at that time, serving a church in Oklahoma; our three children were nearby, including our son who was attending Oklahoma Baptist University (OBU) on a full academic scholarship with a double major in missions and computer science. OBU was only a little more than a two-hour drive from our home. Returning home from a collegiate conference over the Christmas holidays, he told his mother and me he was convinced God wanted him to transfer to a state school where he would have more opportunity to be challenged in his faith and more opportunity to engage in cross-cultural ministry. He was confident God was leading him to a school more than ten hours away from our home.

As his father, I was concerned about his giving up this full scholarship to one of the best Baptist schools in the country. His mother was very concerned about his being so far from home. After some discussion about the wisdom of such a quick decision, only half-jokingly and in frustration, my wife said to him, "Well, who are you going to listen to, God or your mother?" Our son replied quickly and quietly, "What did you raise me to do?" That was the end of that discussion!

Our son attended that school, received a full scholarship there, and found out that they had a computer science department that rivaled Harvard's! He also met his future wife there, who also had surrendered her life to international missions. If our son had not been faithful to the call he received from God to transfer to a new school, he would not have met the wife God had for him! For more than a decade, together they have served in a country closed to the gospel of Jesus with a Muslim people group.

When they left for the missions field for the first time as a young couple, I had a new appreciation for the sacrifice and the support our parents gave us when we moved to New England. What a difficult parting it was! But we knew, as painful as the good-byes were, our son and his wife were doing exactly what God had called them to do. We could not stand in their way. Even through the tears, there was great peace. We knew (and still know) they are in the center of God's will for their lives, and this gives us great joy.

THE STRUGGLE TO SACRIFICE

Ever since Jesus Christ walked on this earth, parents have watched their children take up their crosses daily to follow Jesus. Little is said about the families of the disciples, but most likely, all of those young disciples left behind family members—parents, siblings, and even wives and children perhaps—in obedience to Jesus' call. Peter and Andrew were brothers; both were called by Jesus to leave their fishing enterprise to follow Him and become fishers of men (Matthew 4:18–20). We know Peter was married because Scripture states that his mother-in-law was healed by Jesus (Matthew 8:14–15). James and John, also brothers and fishing partners, left behind their father and what might have been the family business to obey Jesus' call (Matthew 4:21–22). Jesus Himself left mother and siblings to obey His heavenly Father and fulfill the purpose of His earthly life.

Most of what we know about Jesus' mother, Mary, is what we see in the first few chapters of Matthew and Luke. Small glimpses of her life reveal a tension between her loving protectiveness of her son and her joy at seeing her boy Jesus become the man God wanted Him to be as Son of God. In Mark 3:20–35, Mary and her family showed up where Jesus, early in His ministry, had been healing people and dealing with unclean spirits. A ruckus occurred when too many people crowded in to see Jesus at the same time that Jewish legal experts were heatedly accusing Jesus of exorcising demons by Satan's power. Jesus' own family and friends described Jesus as "out of his mind" (v. 21 NIV), "beside himself" (KJV), and having "lost His senses" (NASB). I have sadly met some missionaries whose parents have viewed their children's obedience to God's call with these same assertions. I have prayed with new appointees to world missions fields who stood alone, their parents unwilling to support their surrender to God's call.

God understands the hearts of our missionary parents who struggle to relinquish their children to missions. God relinquished His only Son to the confines of an earthly body and to a death-defying purpose. I do not think it is too radical to say that God the Father missed God the Son in the throne room of heaven for 33 earthly years. Nor is it too radical to say Jesus, Son of man, missed His Father while on earth. How sweet Jesus' early morning prayertimes must have been, those sweet solitary hours of prayer communing with His Father God (Mark 1:35).

Getting back to Jesus' mother, we find Mary with her sister at the foot of the Calvary Cross. That was not the time she let go of her Son;

she actually relinquished her Son to take up His cross in obedience to God at least three years before He carried the old rugged Cross to Calvary. Mary is spotted again in Acts 1:12–14 in the Jerusalem upper room, with her sons, who by then believed, following their elder brother Jesus' ascension. These glimpses reveal the support Jesus' family finally gave Him as His ministry reached its pinnacle and the ultimate sacrifice was given. The greatest fear of any parent is loss of a child. The greatest tragedy of a parent is the death of a child. Our missionary parents grapple with the same fears Mary experienced.

BLESSINGS PARTNERED WITH SACRIFICES

God, our great alleviator of every fear, works in the hearts of missionary parents with a call to a new place of personal surrender and sacrifice. Mary, a missionary mother, told me that through the past 20 years of her daughter's missionary service, "God has partnered blessings with our sacrifices," referring to the sacrifices she and her husband have made as they trusted their daughter to God's call in Southeast Asia.

Talking with Mary, I heard more of the joy she and her husband have experienced with their daughter's missions work than of the sacrifice of long separations and of her empty chair around the family's table for birthdays and holidays. I heard more of that mother's concern for what her daughter had sacrificed—such as her daughter's absence when lifelong friends have died at an early age from cancer or car accidents and her daughter's own accident and subsequent surgery without family to see her through—than of any personal sacrifice. I heard more of a mother's delight in the effective serving of a daughter than of worry over the dangers in hostile areas as Mary shared, "And sometimes it is just hilarious what she does in missions work that I never thought would suit her, like in her first assignment, teaching Vietnamese refugees to drive in the Philippines in preparation to live in the United States." She gave thanks to God for the technology available today that bridges time and distance, enabling them to talk frequently by phone. In the first years of her daughter's service, phone bills for infrequent calls when crises arose ran into the hundreds of dollars; now she pays an affordable monthly rate with unlimited international calls.

Mary tells me she has never experienced regret at God's missionary call to their daughter. All three of her children have been involved in overseas missions—her two sons on volunteer missions teams. She attributes this to having heard God's call on her own life to missions. Looking back, although God did not send her overseas, she is satisfied with God giving her the responsibility and joy of instilling in their three children a responsive heart for missions. Mary takes joy in relinquishing their daughter to God's missions work.

A lesson can be learned from the hearts of our missionary parents. Some of you are rearing the next generation of missionaries. God is at work in you right now preparing you to loosen your grip on their lives so they can be fully obedient to God's leading on a missions path. Think for a moment of your child or your grandchild and the joy you have in them. That joy can never be as great as the joy God had for His Son Jesus when He sent Him on mission to earth or the joy He has in your child right now as that child responds to His call to be on mission in Jesus' name.

Learn from Jim and his wife that God will direct the paths of your children. The path may not seem practical and may take them farther from home than you want, but you will find great joy as they discover the center of God's will for their lives. Learn from Mary and her husband that you have been called to raise your children to hear and respond to God's call to missions. Be encouraged that as you relinquish your child to missions, God will partner great blessings with every sacrifice.

APPLICATION

❧ What, if anything, strikes fear in your heart as you read Mark 10:29–31?

❧ As a parent, describe personal sacrifices God has called you to make on behalf of your children, on behalf of missionary children.

❧ If God is calling your child or grandchild to missions, how is God working in you to help you relinquish them to God's call?

SECTION 3:

Serve

"I press on
to take hold of
that for which
Christ Jesus
took hold of me"

(PHILIPPIANS 3:12).

CHAPTER 15

Surrender, Sacrifice, Serve

B Y NOW, THE QUALITIES OF WHOLEHEARTED LOVE for God with its major elements of personal surrender and living sacrifice and call to serve are scrolling across your mind like images of a computer's screensaver, with ever-moving ribbons of light. No beginning and no ending are seen as the ribbons appear and merge and morph into new designs. The all-for-You life God wants for us is a continuum of holy design: surrender, sacrifice, serve. God wants our life to be so in tune with His that the places where surrender becomes sacrifice and sacrifice becomes serving are a beautiful ever-growing pattern of being the light of Christ in our world.

Paul's letter to the believers at Philippi reminds us that we do not emerge at a particular point on life's timeline fully surrendered:

I want to know Christ—yes, to know the power of his resurrection and participation in his sufferings, becoming like him in his death ... Not that I have already obtained all this, or have already arrived at my goal, but I press on to take hold of that for which Christ Jesus took hold of me.
(PHILIPPIANS 3:10, 12)

Pressing on for Christ Jesus is both puzzling and problematic for new generations of young men and women.

Life presents myriad options of paths to follow: philosophy, religion, culture, lifestyle, a person. From the time of childhood, exposure to these options influences teenagers to make important choices that define their lives as they gain adulthood. When youth choose to be a follower of Jesus Christ, they choose to become His bondservant and press on to take hold of that for which Christ Jesus took hold of them. Or do they?

STARTLING STATISTICS

The Barna Group's church trends research in 2011 tells us, "The Christian community is struggling to remain connected with the next generation of teens and young adults." Their research gives us two startling statistics: "84% of 18- to 29-year-old Christians admit they have no idea how the Bible applies to their field or professional interests, and 59% of millennials with a Christian background have dropped out of church after having gone regularly."

Where is the point of disconnect in young Christian lives that, in time, has widened, becoming a drop-out zone with more questions than answers, more frustration than faith? Is there too small a Christian framework in place in our churches to disciple our youth as they wrestle with identification as Christians? Is there too little courage in youth leadership to look beneath church attendance to heart attendance to the things of Christ? Is there too little importance placed by church and families today on missions discipleship through Acteens® and Challengers® for teenagers in order for them to see their lives as complete only when they live in wholehearted surrender to God as cross-carrying servants of Jesus?

We long for the day when no more people groups will be unreached or unengaged by the gospel of Jesus Christ. The Apostle Paul reminds us in Romans that it takes people with beautiful feet, made beautiful by walking in the steps of Jesus, to accomplish this:

How, then, can they call on the one they have not believed in? And how can they believe in the one of whom they have not heard? And how can they hear without someone preaching to them? And how can anyone preach unless they are sent? As it is written: "How beautiful are the feet of those who bring good news!"
(ROMANS 10:14–15)

With the dropout rate, it will take longer for the qualities of surrender and sacrifice to be a continuum of holy design in young lives; it will take longer for this generation to respond to God's call on their lives to surrender, sacrifice, and serve; and it will take much longer for every nation, tribe, people, and language to hear the gospel.

We can change this trend. As leaders and members in our churches, we can assume our responsibility and step up to be effective leaders and members; we can recommit to the challenge of the WMU® Vision Statement: "Woman's Missionary Union® challenges Christian believers to understand and be radically involved in the mission of God." WMU holds a major key to reversing the dropout rate of millennials and future generations with missions discipleship for every generation.

ROYAL AMBASSADOR ROAD TO SURRENDER

The Apostle Paul gives much guidance for surrender and sacrifice and serving for us and for the beautiful feet of our career missionaries. The world needs more persons like the Apostle Paul, an ambassador for Jesus Christ, to carry the gospel and inspire us to be the same. The world also needs more men like my friend who was a member of Royal Ambassadors® (RA®), a missions organization for boys, as he grew up and who carries the gospel today as a grown-up royal ambassador for Christ. Here is his story:

In a place where Christians are hunted, churches are bombed, nationals are slaughtered for their faith, and foreigners are kidnapped with their children, I have the honor of making Christ known. God placed me overseas working cross-culturally, but it took me a long time to surrender, regardless of risk and potential persecution, to follow His call.

As foreigners, we deal every day with discrimination at military checkpoints along the highways, price gouging in the markets, and the need to constantly watch our backs for one who might follow us home and scout the right time to steal our belongings or, worse, take our lives. Most days seem normal (maybe it's the frog in a boiling pot syndrome). I don't feel or see personal persecution, but the radios, news articles, and prayer requests at a local fellowship keep me reminded of the potential risk. Am I willing to die for Christ? "For to me, to live is Christ and to die is gain" (Philippians 1:21). God's Word through the Apostle Paul rings as a battle cry challenging me to face danger and even death with boldness.

Growing up, I idolized my grandparents' generation who fought in world wars to save our peaceful way of living. I also was a fan of countless superhero movies. As a result, a secular desire lived inside me to triumph through battles and leave my legacy. Thankfully Christ turned this self-glorifying desire into a passion to be Jesus' ambassador in any place, at any cost, thus leaving the legacy of grace through Jesus Christ. Identifying with stories of Jim Elliot, Hudson Taylor, and George Mueller, I eventually became ready to abandon all and pursue a life in cross-cultural ministry, but it did not happen early.

As a young believer, I was the ultimate pretender. I grew into the habit of never committing public secular sins, showing partial attention in church, and never reading my Bible. Thus, without consistent consumption of God's Word, I never grew in faith. My full attention to God became limited to the one week a year I attended Royal Ambassador camp, an outdoor missions education camp for boys. College-age summer staffers invested in my life for a week, walking me through God's Word and challenging me to do what

God says. The summer after fifth grade, I heard God's call to full-time Christian ministry. My inattentive habits the rest of the year kept me from answering this call for many years. As I entered college, my love for RA camp led me to the opportunity to serve on staff. The one week in the year of listening to God became whole summers, and the listening even trickled into the school year. I began to learn a lifestyle of surrender, putting time in God's Word, talking and listening to Him. However, the surrender did not come quickly.

God began to slowly pull me out of the comforts of my Western lifestyle. He asked me to give up some spring break opportunities and Christmas vacations to share Jesus on missions trips in places considered uncomfortable and unreached. It was then I learned about the true joy that comes through true surrender. But still I had a long list of barriers in my heart as to why I would not fully surrender, feeling capable to protect and provide for myself and serve the Lord as I went. I knew I wanted to be able to watch college football every Saturday. I knew that I could not take a family to the bush of Africa because of snakes and disease. I knew that if I did raise a family overseas, that my children would be weird and unaware of secular trends. I knew that I would never get to drive the vehicle I wanted to drive, nor live in the house that I wanted to live in, nor have the career I wanted to have.

These very real barriers hindered me from total surrender. God did me a favor in my moments of partial surrender by sending me all over the world on missions trips and began to remove these barriers one by one. I met missionaries who had hobbies, lived in houses, and had awesome children; but even more so, they lived with true joy because they knew they were following God. He destroyed every single barrier I set up and turned every dream of self-reliance I had sour. He led me to full surrender. I eventually said, "I'll go!" He first sent me for some equipping, so I began to study to make up for the years of habitually never reading my Bible. God's Word did amazing things shaping me to be ready to surrender and go anywhere, even at the risk of serious persecution or death. I was commissioned to serve overseas, but I had more to go to reach full surrender.

God led me to an unreached, unengaged people group in rural Africa—oppressed by Islamic faith, covered in animistic rituals, and also oppressed by a larger, dominant Islamic people group involved in terrorizing a nation to follow its faith. I left my

Western lifestyle passionately ready to carry the good news. I had education and training with plans to lead pockets of believers in sharing their faith with masses of unreached peoples. "For to me, to live is Christ and to die." . . . Wait a minute, this was real! The week I landed, I heard about a pastor in my city who was beheaded. Shortly thereafter, church bombings greatly increased. I attended a small church on Sundays that was great for fellowship and even language study, but I found myself listening for the sound of a car engine on its way to bomb the building more than I did to the sermon. While I adapted to changes in security, I heard stories of attacks of terrorism on schools, government buildings, even on people of their own faith who did not fully agree with their violent method of spreading their religion. Kidnapping and killing of foreigners began. They took children, they showed no mercy, and they promised more to come. I thought of returning home. I wasn't with the people group I came to reach. My plans for engaging were not in motion. Was I prepared for this cost of following Him anywhere?

God sought me in my quiet time, reminding me of my need for Him and His Word, to spend time studying and knowing His Word and living His Word. Reminded of Hebrews 11 and the heroes of the faith, I recalled that not all triumphed on earth. Some suffered for His name, but the world was not worthy of them. I had surrendered and come all across the world to make Him known, but my daily living was reflecting more of my childhood habits: no public sins, partial attention in church, and little attention to God's Word. I had allowed the graphic nature of this new environment to haze my remembrance of true joy that comes through true surrender. I returned from an evacuation, committing again to be His ambassador anytime, anywhere.

Getting to and staying at the point of full surrender is not over. I still live in a place where at any time, as a foreigner, I could be kidnapped, persecuted, or killed, let alone what would be done if they knew my true intentions for making Christ known in their country. I still battle with contentment of living a life of public surrender versus true heart surrender in being willing to follow God wherever He might lead. Abiding in God's Word reminds me of God's sovereignty over these combatants. His Spirit leads me, like it did David and Elijah, to know when to hide in the rocks and when to boldly proclaim the truth to their faces. Daily I have to surrender, not to the fact that I might face the risk of persecution, but to what God has called me to do: to realize that only by grace I was saved, that my people can only be saved through grace in hearing and believing the good news, that for me to live is to make Christ known, and if I'm persecuted or even get to die so others will experience true joy, it's gain! For His glory!

Ira Stanphill wrote the beautiful words of surrender and cross-carrying in his song "Follow Me." His words, "Oh, Jesus, if I die upon a foreign field some day, / 'Twould be no more than love demands, no less could I repay. / . . . But if by death to living they can thy glory see, / I'll take my cross and follow close to thee," paint a picture of the road to full surrender this missionary walks. These words underscore the reality that to be a true servant of God, like this missionary, we too must walk this road and become a living sacrifice for the One who sacrificed His life for all.

APPLICATION

❧ How will this missionary's story help you serve in your church with the millennial generation?

❧ List the names of persons you know who have dropped out of church. Commit to pray for them and be a connector to faith for them.

❧ Where are you on the road to full surrender?

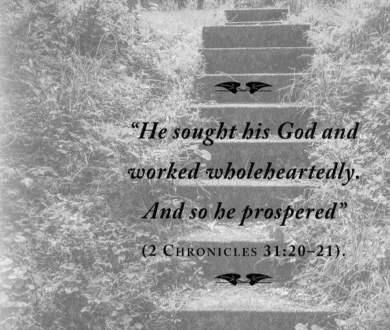

"He sought his God and worked wholeheartedly. And so he prospered"

(2 Chronicles 31:20–21).

CHAPTER 16

The Ins of Wholehearted Serving

❦

OST OF US HAVE A FEW really great moments of serving Jesus in our lifetime. We look back and see the times in which we gave our all to serve at God's call, served with a humble heart, and were faithful and obedient to serve exactly according to God's plan. Oh, that all our serving would shine with these attributes. We are not alone in recognizing these moments, for others affirmed our service and we felt the delight God took in us. When our serving appears dull, we look back again at those shining moments to search for steps to follow or a template to guide us that will enable us to more consistently serve God wholeheartedly. Looking at the life of one of the Old Testament kings provides some advice to help us.

IN SYNC WITH KING HEZEKIAH

King Hezekiah, of King David's dynasty, is known as one of the few great and good kings of Judah; he reigned for 29 years. When he came to the throne at age 25, he had more than one set of king-size footsteps to follow. He chose the godly path of his ancestor King David. He is known for bringing revival to God's people, restoring worship of the one true Jehovah God in the Temple, and setting a high mark of living and serving the God of Israel. King Hezekiah's wholehearted serving is summed up in a passage in 2 Chronicles:

This is what Hezekiah did throughout Judah, doing what was good and right and faithful before the Lord his God. In everything that he undertook in the service of God's temple and in obedience to the law and the commands, he sought his God and worked wholeheartedly. And so he prospered.
(2 Chronicles 31:20–21)

In this summary, we find succinct advice with three ins for whole-hearted serving:

❧ *In Everything:* This in reminds us of the wholeheartedly for God aspect of serving. We serve not from our personal aspirations or by our own initiative, but at the call of God and for His glory. We serve not with our own plans, but according to the will of God. We serve not with our brains or brawn, but with wisdom and strength from God.

❧ *In Service:* We see that Hezekiah, though King of Judah, did not see himself as the linchpin for Judah's revival and recommitment to true worship. Crown or no crown, he saw his work as God's work and himself as a servant. We, too, regardless of position, must be humble servants.

❧ *In Obedience:* The third in confirms God's laws and commands are what constrain and guide our serving. Moreover, no matter how consumed we are in the serving, we must not neglect seeking God daily through time spent in His Word and in prayer. Only then will we be obediently doing what is good and right and faithful.

Ancient King Hezekiah's manner of serving provides good advice for serving wholeheartedly today. Paul reinforced this advice for us: "Serve wholeheartedly, as if you were serving the Lord, not people" (Ephesians 6:7). Most of the work I do—articles for missions resources, assignments to lead a particular conference that focuses on a certain theme, and even this book—I do at the direction of other individuals; however, my goal in everything I do is to serve God wholeheartedly. *The Message* supports a broader understanding with these words:

Servants, respectfully obey your earthly masters but always with an eye to obeying the real master, Christ. Don't just do what you have to do to get by, but work heartily, as Christ's servants doing what God wants you to do. And work with a smile on your face, always keeping in mind that no matter who happens to be giving the orders, you're really serving God.
(EPHESIANS 6:5–7 THE MESSAGE)

Paul gave many ministry and missions assignments to first-century Christians and held them accountable to his expectations. At the same time, he understood a higher call and accountability to God in serving was extended to these men and women in the same measure it was for him. And so is the case for us. Perhaps that is why Paul wrote, "Whatever you do, work at it with all your heart, as working for the Lord, not for human masters" (Colossians 3:23).

A MAN CALLED PETER

Probably, at one time or another, we have all been asked, "Who is your favorite Bible person other than Jesus?" With this question, the lives of many of the women and men of the New Testament and Old Testament parade across my mind. I love Esther for her willingness to be both a living sacrifice as queen to a pagan king and a potential sacrifice for God's people. I admire King David for his brokenheartedness over his sin, and rejoice with him over God's King-size redeeming forgiveness. The story of Daniel's unswerving faithfulness to God, despite the threat and punishment of being thrown into a den of lions, inspires me to take a strong stand for my God in today's world. The story of Mary's heart for God and her song, the Magnificat, reminds me to trust God in all things and to rejoice in His love for me.

But then there is Peter. We have heard so many Peter stories of impulsivity, brashness, and words he wished he could take back: from a walking-on-water-in-faith story to a three-denial, rooster-crowing story; all the stories in Peter's life between some of the first words he heard from Jesus, "Come, follow me" (Mark 1:17), and final words from Jesus to him, "You must follow me" (John 21:22). So, if by *favorite,* the person who asks the question means who has impacted my spiritual life the most, teaching me through example about God's grace and mercy and love, my answer is Peter. If the asker means who has spurred me on to a deeper understanding of Jesus and living for Jesus, my answer is still Peter.

My favorite is not just the disciple Peter who abandoned his nets and walked for three years with Jesus, but the evangelist Peter who preached and 3,000 came to faith in Christ; the Apostle Peter who, with his life on the line, could not help speaking about all he had seen and heard; and the letter-writer Peter, who understood the call to be a suffering servant like Jesus, following in the steps of Jesus. He wrote, "To this you were called, because Christ suffered for you, leaving you an example, that you should follow in his steps" (1 Peter 2:21).

IN HIS STEPS

King Hezekiah gave us three *ins* for serving. Peter provided us four *in* steps. He gave us guidance from the viewpoint of one who had seen the Calvary Cross carried and the perfect sacrifice made.

The first step is *in holiness.* Peter wrote, "But just as he who called you is holy, so be holy in all you do; for it is written: 'Be holy, because

I am holy'" (1 Peter 1:15–16). Peter does not ease believers into holiness and does not make it optional. He presents serving in holiness as the command from God that it is. Five times in Leviticus, God commanded His people to be holy as He gave them the laws that would guide their lives. Did Peter struggle with being holy? Knowing all his stories from the gospels, we can respond, "Yes!" Do we struggle with being holy? Another collective response is likely, "Yes!" The J. B. Phillips New Testament tells us in this 1 Peter 1 passage that holiness is for "every department of your lives," going on to suggest God has the right to command us to be holy as we serve because we are redeemed servants, ransomed by a great price: "The price was in fact the life-blood of Christ, the unblemished and unstained lamb of sacrifice" (v. 19 Phillips). Our only acceptable response to God's call to be holy is, "Yes, Lord!"

Second, as we serve in holiness, we should also serve *in reverent fear* of our Lord who has called us and redeemed us. Peter instructed, "Since you call on a Father who judges each person's work impartially, live out your time as foreigners here in reverent fear" (1 Peter 1:17). We are simply sojourners on earth, but sojourners with a call to kingdom purposes. As close as Peter was to Jesus, one of the inner circle of Jesus' disciples, he had learned the lesson of reverence for God. In all the ways we serve God, we must never be casual or callous about serving, but always aware of the privilege we have of being called by Jesus to leave our nets and follow Him, in His steps. Peter, with his own past irreverent denial of Jesus having been forgiven, reminds us we are to serve with reverent respect for Almighty God in every department of our lives.

The third of Peter's *in* steps is found in this verse: "To this you were called, because Christ suffered for you, leaving you an example, that you should follow *in his steps*" (1 Peter 2:21; italics added). As mentioned in chapter 9, Charles Sheldon authored the challenging discipleship book *In His Steps* in 1897. This novel presents the story of a community challenged by their pastor to do nothing without first asking, "What would Jesus do?" This question inspired readers to adopt that same question for their Christian walk. The book is considered a classic today for its ability to still shake up one's view of what it means to be a follower of Jesus. It is the source for the popular, and perhaps faddish, What would Jesus do? motto of evangelical Christianity in the 1990s. A youth group at Calvary Reformed Church in Michigan studied Charles Sheldon's book and began using the *WWJD* acronym for this question as they pledged to apply it to their decision making. They had cloth bracelets made with *WWJD* on them to wear as reminders of their belief in God's call to follow in Jesus' steps and to choose to do as Jesus did, loving and serving others in the name of Jesus. They did not know their pledge and bracelet would sweep the nation and the world with reminders to serve Jesus, following in His steps.

Peter's fourth in step is *"in the grace and knowledge of our Lord and Savior Jesus Christ"* (2 Peter 3:18). No greater support exists for serving the Lord than experiencing Jesus' grace and learning more about Him. Effective Bible study teachers say they receive the greatest blessing from the lesson because of their time studying in preparation. They also know more can be gleaned from the Scripture passages, so much more can be learned about the things of our Lord than the time in the classroom allows. We must never be so immersed in the actions of serving that our spiritual growth is relegated to an hour a week or completely neglected. We must never become so committed to tasks that we set aside our personal need to grow closer and more knowledgeable of the things and ways of Jesus Christ. Wholehearted serving in His steps is only possible through time spent deep in God's Word and devoted to prayer so we will continue to grow in the grace and knowledge of our Lord Jesus Christ. Only then will our hearts be filled with God's Spirit and our service bring glory to the name of Jesus.

APPLICATION

❧ How will you apply the three *ins* from King Hezekiah's serving?

❧ Who is your favorite Bible person? What has this person's life taught you?

❧ How will you follow Jesus in His steps using the four *ins* Peter shared?

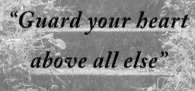

"Guard your heart

above all else"

(Proverbs 4:23).

CHAPTER 17

Servant Hearts

*T*HE FACT THAT JESUS INVITES US to follow Him in His holy footsteps should stop us in our tracks. This invitation is not for those with a heart full of pride grasping for blessings. It is an invitation to surrender, sacrifice, and serve with servant hearts.

In my New Hampshire years, I was privileged to sing in a women's trio. Cheryl, Jean, and I chose the name Servant Hearts for our trio out of a desire that our music be for the glory of God and point others to serving Him. Jean, as soprano and organizer of our trio, chose our music, whereas Cheryl and I chimed in with the harmonies. We loved meeting together to pore over Jean's newest music choices, to sing and pray together, and then to sing whenever asked, serving the Lord in song. Those were a few very special years singing together and giving God the glory for His gifts of friendship and voices blended to serve Him.

Giving all the glory to God in serving is possible only when we attend to the heart matter of guarding our hearts, guarding them from the sins of pride, greed, and superiority. God's Word advises us, "Guard your heart above all else, for it determines the course of your life" (Proverbs 4:23 NLT). Unguarded hearts lead us off the path of Jesus' footsteps onto a compromised course. At first, our steps may seem only a slight deviation, mostly a parallel path of needing the approval and affirmation from others. But soon acclaim in the church and applause in the community can weaken the protection of our hearts. Sins of pride, greed, and superiority can attack weakened hearts and cause them to assume this praise is for us because of some inborn talent, a finely honed skill, or even our fervent faith. Where in any of this is there room for giving God the glory when we seek after and bask in self-glory?

When a person's path angles sharply away from the footsteps of Jesus, self-glory can lead to the slippery slope of carnal sin that too often has caused headlines to scream the secret sins of Christians. The world loves to see Jesus' followers fall and Satan enjoy a victory. But God does not! Nor does Jesus. Their hearts hurt when we fall (Ephesians 4:30). Jesus' heart grieves when we let down the guard He has put around our heart and we, His followers, fall into sin. Jesus prayed in the garden, "Protect them by the power of your name," even lamenting the one lost, "doomed to destruction so that Scripture would be fulfilled" Judas (John 17:11–12). Jesus knew there would be great temptations living in this world; He knew there would be guard-lowering failures given the frailty of man and the free choice we have. Jesus knew there would even be the temptation for self-glorifying service in ministry. God said, "I will not yield my glory to another" (Isaiah 48:11). When we worship the acclaim we receive more than the Lord we proclaim in word, deed, or song, it is sin. How then do we guard our hearts?

HEARTS GUARDED BY PEACE

The reality is, we do not do the guarding. The peace of God is what guards our hearts and minds: "And the peace of God, which transcends all understanding, will guard your hearts and your minds in Christ Jesus" (Philippians 4:7). But we must accept our responsibility to seek God's peace, which can be accessed, put in place, and maintained only through the power of prayer. Great men and women of the Bible knew the key to selflessly serving God was found in prayer. Prayer began in the garden with pure communion as Adam and Eve walked and talked with God. But prayer took on new characteristics after sin entered mankind; prayer became the bridge between our mortality and

God's eternality. Instead of comfortable sinless communion, prayer became an act of kneeling, prostrating, and stretching up hands to God for forgiveness, supplication, and praise.

The prayers we find in Scripture have been studied, preached, and prayed by Christians for centuries. Their promises have been claimed for our own heart needs. We find in the Bible prayers of petition as Abram (Abraham) questioned what God could do for him since he had no child (Genesis 15:2–3) and as Hannah wept and prayed for a son (1 Samuel 1:10–11); prayers of intercession by Samuel for the nation of Israel (1 Samuel 7:5–9) and by Paul for the Ephesian believers (Ephesians 3:14–21); desperate prayers for courage alluded to by Esther (Esther 4:15–16) and for strength voiced by Samson (Judges 16:28); and penitent prayers for forgiveness by David (Psalm 51) and by the thief on the cross (Luke 23:42). Prayer, then and now, is the common denominator in the lives of God's servants whose hearts have been guarded by the unsurpassed peace of God.

Billy Graham, one of the most respected and influential evangelists of modern times, has been called God's ambassador, evangelist extraordinaire, and pastor to presidents. How did he consistently follow in the footsteps of Jesus without succumbing to the praise and adulation of twentieth- and twenty-first-century Christians and the leaders of nations of our world? We see a clue to this in an observation made by Graham:

The men upon whose shoulders rested the initial responsibility of Christianizing the world came to Jesus with one supreme request. [See Luke 11:1.] They did not say, "Lord, teach us to preach"; "Lord, teach us to do miracles"; or "Lord, teach us to be wise"... but they said, "Lord, teach us to pray."

Billy Graham knew well the need for time spent on his knees in prayer to know God in a deeper way, to access the power of God for the task of evangelizing the modern world, and to keep strong the guard on his heart from the Prince of Peace.

THE LORD DIRECTS HIS STEPS

Humble walks in the footsteps of Jesus are not the predominant life-style in the Los Angeles area of California. Humility is seldom seen on the red carpet of Academy Awards nights, on the late-night talk shows, or in the concert halls. But it is seen in the life of a new church planter who has taken up his cross to follow Jesus in a new direction. God has called Scott Wesley Brown to be a North American Mission Board church planter apprentice in Southern California.

For more than three decades, Scott Wesley Brown, a Christian recording artist and church worship leader, has faithfully proclaimed the message of Jesus. His concert ministry has taken him to more than 50 countries and every state in the United States. His mission of providing musical instruments and training for Christian musicians in third-world countries has made him one of the most influential Christian recording artists worldwide.

But a church planter instead of a music leader? Scott wondered. Citing, "The mind of man plans his way, but the Lord directs his steps" (Proverbs 16:9 NASB), Scott says as he began to hear the call to church planting, away from leading music in a church, he pictured in his mind the Malibu beach area with his children living nearby, the support of a well-known Christian actor who wanted to see a church started there, and a local pastor encouraging him. But God had another plan. Scott has followed Jesus' footsteps and finds himself "smack dab in the middle of the motion picture and television industry!" He describes the location: "Around the corner and in walking distance from our new church, Fellowship Church, is NBC, Universal, the Cartoon Network, Nickelodeon, Disney Studios, DreamWorks, and a host of other famous film studios and production houses."

In addition to the workplaces of artists and those in the film and television industry, housing with many such persons is nearby. Behind the new church site are a retired artist's colony and an apartment complex that houses many who work in the elements of these entertainment companies.

"It can be tough to be a Christian in this industry," states Scott. "We want to create an environment where poets and songwriters, painters and sculptors, artists of all types can express their God-inspired talents." The new church's focus is on being a missional church, impacting the unchurched and the lost for Jesus, and seeping into every crack and crevice of the world around them. Scott Wesley Brown and his wife, Belinda, have followed Jesus' footsteps to minister to the artistic community in Southern California with their personal understanding of the challenges, the dreams, and the spiritual needs.

In the culture of artists striving for recognition and significance, what will guard Scott's and Belinda's hearts? It will not be spiritually creating a chain-link fence of good intentions to stay on their new path, nor will it be the electric fence jolts of activity in striving for success in God's kingdom work. It will be the peace of God they find through daily personal prayer. "And the peace of God, which transcends all understanding, will guard your hearts and your minds in Christ Jesus" (Philippians 4:7).

GUARDING TARGETED SERVANT HEARTS

"Tinker, tailor, soldier, sailor, rich man, poor man, beggar man, thief," the nursery rhyme to determine who is "It," reminds us that regardless of who we are, what our job is, where we live, or when we began to follow Jesus, sometimes we are "It." Sometimes we are targeted and tempted by Satan; the guard of peace around our heart is assaulted to weaken our witness and our serving.

Paul knew the resourcefulness of Satan to attack our minds as well as our hearts, so he wrote in the following verses what God wants to be our focus:

Finally, brothers and sisters, whatever is true, whatever is noble, whatever is right, whatever is pure, whatever is lovely, whatever is admirable—if anything is excellent or praiseworthy—think about such things. Whatever you have learned or received or heard from me, or seen in me—put it into practice. And the God of peace will be with you. (PHILIPPIANS 4:8–9)

The invitation to follow in Jesus' footsteps is for those whose hearts and minds are filled with these things. How can we be surrendered and sacrificial of heart and mind to serve if our ereaders and bookshelves are cluttered with books that lack truth, nobility, and purity; or if the movies and television programs we watch are neither excellent nor praiseworthy in our Christian context; and a desire for more overflow our homes, our closets, and our jewelry boxes while our giving to missions offerings is less each year? And how can the heart and mind focus of our church be admirably missional if its giving to the Cooperative Program is decreased, diverted to in-church needs or to make our buildings more expansive and our events more extrav gant? We cannot.

To live with a servant heart in the footsteps of Jesus, we cannot look back with "been there, done that" attitudes toward surrender and sacrifice. When the Spirit of God nudges us to reexamine the peace guard He has placed around our heart and when one Scripture after another points to surrender and sacrifice, it is time to take a spiritual inventory of our hearts and minds, our homes, and our churches to verify we are still operating with the heart of a servant.

APPLICATION

❧ Describe how it feels to be invited to follow with your footsteps in the exact footsteps of Jesus?

❧ What do you need to change in your prayer life to have a servant heart, your heart and mind guarded by God's peace?

❧ Do an inventory of your home to see what needs to be removed, given away, or reevaluated so that you may fill your heart and mind with what is admirable to Jesus.

"Solomon stood before the altar of the LORD in front of the whole assembly of Israel, spread out his hands toward heaven and said: LORD, the God of Israel, there is no God like you in heaven above or on earth below—you who keep your covenant of love with your servants who continue wholeheartedly in your way"

(1 KINGS 8:22–23).

CHAPTER 18

And Solomon Prayed: Prayer Pattern for Intercession

A GUARDED HEART UNDERSTANDS both the privilege and the responsibility of prayer. It beats to the cadence of "For God so loved the world" and "whoever believes" (John 3:16). We think of Solomon as a great and wise king. But do we think of him as a praying king? We should. Solomon was a son of David, the third king of Israel, and the builder of the Temple; he understood prayer and knew intercession is a key part of praying for others to live wholeheartedly. First Kings 8 contains the blessing- and prayer-filled account of the dedication of the Temple, which was built according to detailed instructions for the glory of the name of the Lord God. When it was completed, the whole assembly of Israel gathered and the ark of the Lord was brought into the inner sanctuary. As the priests withdrew, the glory of God filled the Temple like a cloud.

Visualize this "God with us" moment in time: The Temple, with its inner courts, cedar columns and paneling, carvings of palms and cherubim, gold overlays, bronze stands and basins, and ten pure gold lampstands, has been completed. Then the glory of the Lord entered and filled the Temple. As you see this in your mind, do you hear the sounds of choirs singing: "The LORD is in his holy temple: let all the earth keep silence before him" (Habakkuk 2:20 KJV)? Into this holy hush response to God's presence walked Solomon, king of Israel, to bring the blessing on God's people. Following the blessing, "Solomon stood before the altar of the LORD in front of the whole assembly of Israel, spread out his hands toward heaven and said: 'LORD, the God of Israel, there is no God like you in heaven above or on earth below— you who keep your covenant of love with your servants who continue wholeheartedly in your way'" (1 Kings 8:22–23). Take a few moments and let the presence of our holy, loving God enfold you.

KING-SIZE PRAYER PATTERN

We see from Solomon's prayer that he got it about wholehearted living and knew a key component to wholehearted living is the prayer support of intercessors. That day, the day God's glory filled the Temple, King Solomon prayed a glorious prayer for the people of Israel to live wholeheartedly. His prayer of intercession touched on God's promises; sin and forgiveness; judgment and vindication; defeat by enemies and victorious return to the land; drought and rain; and disaster, disease, and God's forgiveness, again, and action with a stated desired result: "so that they will fear you [the LORD, God of Israel]" (1 Kings 8:40). And further, Solomon prayed for the foreigner who would come to seek the Lord. He prayed that the Lord would do what the seeker requested for this purpose: "so that all the peoples of the earth may know your name and fear you, as do your own people Israel" (v. 43). In Solomon's prayer, we see a pattern for intercessory prayer.

❧ In his great understanding of God's plan for redemption and for governing His people, Solomon prayed the promise of God to maintain descendants of David on Israel's throne. God's Word is filled with promises we, too, can pray as we intercede for others.

❧ In his great wisdom and seemingly prophetic insight, Solomon did not pray for easing or removal of God's discipline, but for God to hear the pleas of His people when they repented amid the suffering for their sinfulness. As intercessors, we are not to pray for God to remove the pain of sin in those we love, but to pray they will turn to God from their suffering in full repentance.

❧ In sincerity, Solomon prayed for judgment and vindication. We, too, can pray for justice and truthfulness to always prevail. Today's divisions in families, churches, and governments need our prayers for this.

❧ In his awareness that battles would come from enemies, Solomon prayed for protection and victory for God's people. Today's Christians face battles: spiritual, social, and physical battles. We, too, should pray for God's protection for fellow Christians and for God's victory to be gained.

❧ In touch with the reality of the Israelites, Solomon prayed again for their most pressing needs: sinfulness and the need for forgiveness. We should pray for the real and pressing issues in the lives of those God places on our hearts. Rather than just asking, "God bless," we need to pray specifically, as did Solomon.

❧ In hope for the world, Solomon prayed for the nations of the world to come to Jehovah, the one true God. We are the worldwide intercessors for missionaries, people groups, cultures, and leaders of nations that they would come to know the only way to God, Jesus Christ.

PRAYER PATTERN FROM WEST AFRICA

Mary Slessor knew about prayer. A young, single Scottish missionary, she sailed through the Atlantic to Africa in 1876, making her way inland. As her ship sailed into the mouth of the Calabar River, she arrived at a place that was home to man-eating lions, death-delivering armies of insects, snakes, as well as tribes engaged in witchcraft and fearsome practices. Called Duke Town, later Calabar, Nigeria, had become a bastion for Atlantic slave trade. Into this spiritual darkness stepped the young Mary, supported by those holding the ropes of prayer for her mission. Perhaps she, like countless of the modern missions movement, borrowed words of missionary William Carey as she prepared to leave home: "I will go down, if you will hold the ropes."

Mary worked in the town and in the nearby villages, teaching, providing medical care, and preaching Jesus. She strived to dispel tribal practices of killing a man's wives when he died so he would not be alone in death and of killing newborn twins, which superstition held to be bringers of plague. Her courage to venture far inland to reach remote villages with the gospel, her ability to help to bring peace when hostilities between tribes arose, and her dedicated love for all the tribal people earned her the name White Mother. Mary said, "Prayer is the greatest power God has put into our hands for service—praying is harder than doing, at least I find it so, but the dynamic lies that way to advance the Kingdom."

Every evangelical missions society has produced men and women like Mary Slessor, who, in their desire to serve wholeheartedly, have discovered prayer is their lifeline. God did not leave them alone to pray. He called into His prayer-receiving throne room others to be their "rope holders," their intercessors who faithfully kneel in prayer to lift them up to the Father. Think about the missionaries for whom you pray each day, their smiling faces on missionary picture prayer cards posted on your refrigerator or tucked into your Bible. Visualize your intercessory prayers connecting with their prayers at the feet of Jesus. Think about the unknown faces of names and initials you read on the prayer calendar and yourself in heaven's throne room before the Father with each of these missionary brothers and sisters. See that meeting as your hearts joined in one heart in communion with Christ. Charles Spurgeon, preaching on the topic of intercessory prayer, had this to say to his congregation:

Intercession should throb like a pulse through the whole body, causing every living member to feel the sacred impulse. Intercession is one of the least things which we can do, and yet it is one of the greatest: let us not be slack in it.

MISSIONARY PARENT PRAYER PATTERN

Parents are fervent intercessors for their missionary children and grandchildren. Conversations with a previously mentioned missionary mother (see chap. 14.) about her daughter are peppered with the prayers she offers for her daughter, who is on the other side of the world, working with Muslim women and children to share the love of Jesus. Although her daughter has said, "Don't pray for my safety; pray I would be bold," this mother, also named Mary, prays for both with confidence that God will do both. She adds to her prayers for boldness a request for a good measure of wisdom, praying her daughter will recognize "people of peace" and will be kept from those who would harm her because of her faith. Her prayers have broadened to include the people her daughter serves and the people that the mother herself now meets in her own community with ties to her daughter's city and country of service. And finally, Mary prays, "I don't know her needs today, but You do and have promised to supply all her needs." Listen to Mary's praying heart through her story:

As the mother of a single young lady serving as a career apprentice in a South Asian country, I have learned this past year that I can love and pray for my daughter, but only God can really take care of her, giving her comfort, strength, and hope in hard or sad times. No matter how old your child is, you still want to "fix" everything for them. God has given me the assurance that she is really in His care "for such a time as this" [see Esther 4:14]. Over and over this year, He has allowed me to see He is putting people in her life that can be there when I cannot be. I am so thankful for other personnel who surround her with love and encouragement.

Prayers can be spoken even when the words needed are not known to the person praying. Many times, I just have to say, "Please, dear Jesus, take care of my daughter in all that she may encounter, whether it is illness, dangers, loneliness, language studies, or all the unknowns that I can't even begin to imagine." I am encouraged by all the people who tell me they pray for her every day, sometimes people I don't even know. God is good all the time, as her dad said many times before his death.

Ever since she was a little girl, she wanted to be a missionary. Her testimony speaks of the importance of Mission Friends®, GA®, and camp in her life. Early on, she was interested in the people and the stories of other countries. It is a comfort that her daddy knew before he died she would soon be a missionary. I am thankful we have the wonderful world of Skype to communicate. I can see her flat, her friends, her house church, and so much more of her everyday life several times a week. This is another way God comforts both of us.

Our daughter is our Samuel, a miracle baby after about eight years of praying! I've always felt [God] had special plans for her life. We have loved the verse Jeremiah 29:11 ["'For I know the plans I have for you,' declares the Lord, 'plans to prosper you and not to harm you, plans to give you hope and a future.'"] and rested in its promise for our children and ourselves. It is a great reminder for me to trust her to His care daily. I don't know if the correct word is sacrifice; God gave us our wonderful daughter as His gift we can now share with the world as she serves to reach the nations. This brings joy to my praying heart!

WMU PRAYER PATTERNS

Prayer for our missionaries is the heartbeat of Woman's Missionary Union. From the organizational days of 1888, any time and anywhere WMU has met, so have hearts and hands met in prayer for our missionaries. From the missionary prayer card of Annie Armstrong's first days in office as corresponding secretary of national WMU, auxiliary to Southern Baptist Convention (SBC), to the Prayer Patterns of today's *Missions Mosaic*, WMU members have been guided to intercede for our missionaries. In 1952, WMU's listing of missionaries was presented in calendar format and has continued in this way for prayer for our missionaries on their birthdays.

As I visit with missionaries where they serve or with missionaries on stateside assignment, I repeatedly hear words to this effect: "Thank you for your prayers. If it were not for WMU's prayer support, we could not stay and serve. Please do not stop praying." Their words call to mind words of Samuel: "Far be it from me that I should sin against the LORD by failing to pray for you" (1 Samuel 12:23).

In these days of great challenges and mounting dangers for our missionaries, with still-to-be-reached people groups and with places where Jesus has never been worshipped, how can we not be a missions praying people? We must never relinquish this privilege; we must purpose to pray daily and devotedly for our missionaries. Wesley L. Duewel, who served as a missionary for 25 years in India and then as president for One Mission Society, said, "Prayer is the supreme way to be workers together with God." How can we not be praying colaborers with God?

WMU's historic watchword is 1 Corinthians 3:9 (KJV): "For we are labourers together with God." Our mandate, our call, is to labor on our knees for our colaborers.

This intercessory prayer laboring was not meant to be simple and without a strain on the heart. This level of praying is much more than a whispered sentence or two. Duewel noted in his book, *Touch the World Through Prayer*, the type of prayer that moves God:

Heaven pays little attention to casual requests. God is not moved by feeble desires, listless prayers, and spiritual laziness. God rejoices to see a soul on fire with holy passion as the heart reaches out to Him.

Now is the time to restore passionate, on-our-knees, weeping prayer for the lost of the world and those who have gone to bring the light of Jesus to them.

APPLICATION

❧ In what way did God speak to you as you revisited God's presence in Solomon's dedication of the Temple?

❧ How will Solomon's prayers impact your praying for others?

❧ What will you glean from the discussion of Mary Slessor's life, missionary mother Mary's testimony, and the quotes of Wesley Duewel that will help you be an effective and passionate intercessor for our missionaries?

Conclusion

*"But be sure to fear the
LORD and serve him
faithfully with all your
heart; consider what great
things he has done for you"*

(1 SAMUEL 12:24).

CHAPTER 19

Final Wholehearted Words

W̶E ARE LABORERS TOGETHER WITH GOD. We are His colaborers with our hearts lifted to Him in surrender, with our minds submitted to His will in sacrifice, and with our hands and feet obedient to Him to serve. Surrender, sacrifice, serve—these are the key components of wholehearted living for God. Let us look at another Scripture to keep us focused on living wholeheartedly: "But be sure to fear the LORD and serve him faithfully with all your heart; consider what great things he has done for you" (1 Samuel 12:24).

Everyone loves Samuel. He was birthed from answered prayer out of a barren womb; was dedicated to serve God from a young tender age; heard and obeyed the call of God to be judge, priest, and prophet; and transitioned God's people from a loosely governed nation to a monarchy. Samuel's faithfulness kept him living wholeheartedly for God and put him on the heart of the author of Hebrews as he wrote him into the Hall of Faith (Hebrews 11:32).

The words of Samuel to God's people in 1 Samuel 12 (NIV) are subtitled, "Samuel's Farewell Speech"; they were his swan song that defined his last years as God's servant. Last words recorded for history are often significant words that deserve our attention. This time of Samuel's life may not be as familiar to us as other times, but as we look at it, we see much to consider that reflects Samuel's history with God's people, who have cycled in and out of faithfulness and rebellion, whining and celebrating, victory and defeat.

KING OR NO KING

The Israelites wanted a king. We can imagine what their whine might have been: "Other nations have kings. Why cannot we have a king too?" But God was their King. Why didn't they see this? They chose to be ruled by an earthly fallible, prone-to-wander human king over eternal infallible, faithful God. Did they know themselves so well they thought a human king would not see all their weaknesses and wickedness and would keep them from punishment through battle defeats and enslavement? We know how that worked out; it did not.

This desire for a king should never have been an issue for God's chosen people. This request again reflects man's desire for self-determination. God relented and gave them the king they wanted. But God was still in control, as we see in 1 Samuel 12, for He was the King over earthly King Saul.

"But when you saw that Nahash king of the Ammonites was moving against you, you said to me, 'No, we want a king to rule over us'—even though the LORD your God was your king. Now here is the king you have chosen, the one you asked for; see, the LORD has set a king over you. If you fear the LORD and serve and obey him and do not rebel against his commands, and if both you and the king who reigns over you follow the LORD your God—good! But if you do not obey the LORD, and if you rebel against his commands, his hand will be against you, as it was against your ancestors."
(1 Samuel 12:12–15)

God held His people and King Saul accountable to fear Him, serve and obey Him, live by His commands, and follow Him (v. 14). *The Message* gives us Samuel's warning with these words: "But if you don't obey him and rebel against what he tells you, king or no king, you will fare no better than your fathers" (v. 15).

At times, our surrendered hearts whine a little and the words *I want* or *I deserve* tremble on our lips. Our wants overcome our contentment in sacrifice. Our joy in serving is stolen by a desire that grows. Sometimes a storm of life is required for God to get our attention and make a midcourse correction to return us to living wholeheartedly for Him, our King.

To help the Israelites realize God's displeasure with their request for a king, Samuel prayed for a miraculous thunder and rainstorm— at the end of the dry season, at that! God brought the miracle that same day.

"I will call on the LORD to send thunder and rain. And you will realize what an evil thing you did in the eyes of the LORD when you asked for a king." Then Samuel called on the LORD, and that same day the LORD sent thunder and rain. So all the people stood in awe of the LORD and of Samuel.
(1 SAMUEL 12:17–18)

I wonder, *Did the clouds slowly gather on the western horizon, growing darker, becoming laced with flashes of lightning, and sending out reverberating sounds of thunder as the storm approached? Or did the clouds suddenly cover the ripened wheat fields and that out-in-the-open gathering place, threatening the lives of the persons there as well as their harvest?*

This storm, regardless of how it came about, convicted the Israelites of God's displeasure with their king-size, sin-initiated request. Fear overcame their stricken hearts, and they turned to Samuel, begging him to intercede with God for their lives.

Some storms of life are God created to bring us to our knees in repentance. Some storms of life are not of God but have been allowed by God to draw us closer to Him and achieve purposes we cannot yet see. But all storms are catalysts for remembering that God has promised never to leave us and has proven Himself faithful throughout our lives.

CONTINUE PRAYING AND TEACHING

Samuel assured the repentant people they would not be rejected by God, not because of anything they had done for good, but because of God's own great name, Covenant Keeper. Samuel pledged to continue being their intercessory prayer partner and teacher. The depth of Samuel's obedience to God and commitment to serve Him shows up in this verse: "As for me, far be it from me that I should sin against the LORD by failing to pray for you. And I will teach you the way that is good and right" (1 Samuel 12:23).

GO FORWARD!

With the sounds of joy and remembrances still in the air from two years of celebrating the 125th anniversary of national WMU, it is fitting to look back at leaders final words calling us to surrender, sacrifice, and serve.

Annie Armstrong, first corresponding secretary, who taught us to say with her, "Go Forward!" neared death as national WMU celebrated its 50th anniversary. From her bed, she sent these commanding final words to the assembled women: "After the study of God's Word comes study of the fields, then people pray, then they give. . . . 'Speak unto the children of Israel, that they go forward'" (referring to Exodus 14:15). Our organization has stayed true to these founding principles of biblically sound missions education and mission support. As Samuel did not fail to pray for and to teach the Israelites, Annie Armstrong did not fail to pray for and to teach others to stay true to God's plan.

WALK IN WHOLEHEARTED OBEDIENCE

Now let us return to God's Word for more examples of final words.

Israel's second king was David; he had many spiritual ups and downs during his reign over Israel. His last words, somewhat reminiscent of Samuel's, were spoken to his son and future king of Israel, Solomon, with wholehearted language:

"I am about to go the way of all the earth," he said. "So be strong, act like a man, and observe what the Lord *your God requires: Walk in obedience to him, and keep his decrees and commands, his laws and regulations, as written in the Law of Moses. Do this so that you may prosper in all you do and wherever you go and that the* Lord *may keep his promise to me: 'If your descendants watch how they live, and if they walk faithfully before me with all their heart and soul, you will never fail to have a successor on the throne of Israel.'"*
(1 Kings 2:2–4)

David wanted his son to have a heart for God, to be a better-than-he-was man after God's own heart. He knew from his own roller-coaster ride, with reckless failures and renewed fervor for God, that walking faithfully before God was a heart and soul matter. His last words to his son were about wholehearted obedience.

BRING BEST SERVICE FOR BEST KING

Fannie E. S. Heck, second president of the national missions organization where I serve, was one of the most quoted presidents. Her official last words are some of her most memorable words and reflect her all-for-You heart. Beginning with, "See to it only, that you listen to His voice and follow only where Christ leads," she closed with the following:

Bring all your best powers into the best service of the best King. Thus shall your work abide and be abundantly blessed of God to your own joy and the joy of the world. In the belief that you will continue to adorn the doctrine of service, I bid you dear friends, farewell. The God whom we love and serve will keep His own in love and peace and finally through His great love wherewith He hath loved us bring us all rejoicing into His presence above. Most earnestly I pray—God be with you till we meet again.

Fannie Heck was well aware that we need no king but King Jesus!

FINISH STRONG

Paul wrote his last words in a second recorded letter to Timothy from behind the bars of a Roman prison, his execution date looming. The entire letter is one of final instructions and encouragement for his protégé and "son" Timothy, who was pastoring the church at Ephesus. Imagine how precious these last words from Paul were for Timothy. We can picture Timothy reading this letter from his beloved mentor, his tears brimming and falling to the parchment as he reads the words and then reads them again:

For I am already being poured out like a drink offering, and the time for my departure is near. I have fought the good fight, I have finished the race, I have kept the faith. Now there is in store for me the crown of righteousness, which the Lord, the righteous Judge, will award to me on that day— and not only to me, but also to all who have longed for his appearing. (2 TIMOTHY 4:6–8)

Paul, by example, encouraged Timothy to fight a good fight, finish strong, and keep the faith.

FAITHFULLY PRAY

Alma Hunt, beloved national WMU executive secretary 1948–74, in her final Annual Meeting speech, said, "I have been aware every day that my life has been linked with yours that I have spent my energies in what I believe to be the greatest work on earth." She shared stories from her years of serving in her entertaining and enlightening book *Reflections from Alma Hunt*, revealing her all-for-You life. She concluded the book with a prayer she offered that was included in the records of the meeting. She brought her reflections to a close with her prayer, saying, "It continues to be my prayer."

Oh, God, may these women created in Your own image, gifted with potential by You, chosen to give to this generation a faithful accounting of Your will, be able to contribute mightily. May they move churches to see farther and to reach higher than those who have gone before us were able to do. Oh, God, help these women to give of their very best. Help them to lean heavily on You, that the years ahead may be full of Your glory. Amen.

Alma Hunt's faithful praying, like Samuel's, continued to bless Christ followers until God called her heavenward in her 98th year.

LAST WORDS OF JESUS: BE MY WITNESSES

Jesus' last words are most often thought of as His words from the Cross. However, Jesus' very last words on this earth are found in Luke's second writing, the Book of Acts.

He said to them: "It is not for you to know the times or dates the Father has set by his own authority. But you will receive power when the Holy Spirit comes on you; and you will be my witnesses in Jerusalem, and in all Judea and Samaria, and to the ends of the earth."
(ACTS 1:7–8)

Like a sequel to the life and ministry of Jesus, Acts tells the story of the Holy Spirit–anointed apostles taking to heart Jesus' very last words. Chapter by chapter, we see the apostles' complete surrender to Jesus' last words, their personal sacrifice to spread the gospel of Jesus, and their wholehearted serving in obedience to their Lord. As the apostles were blessed by these words and commanded by these words, so too are we as recipients of the Holy Spirit and followers of the risen Christ.

We each have only one life to offer Jesus our Lord and King. What will our final words be at the close of our life? Will they reflect a life surrendered completely to Jesus? Will our final words be of the joy of giving our all as a living sacrifice? Will they be an encouragement to others to serve the Lord with all their heart, soul, and mind until Jesus returns? Will they reveal an all-for-You life?

APPLICATION

❧ How will these final words of God's Bible heroes spur you on to live wholeheartedly?

❧ How will these final words of these legends spur you on to serve in your place of ministry or work?

❧ How will these final words of Jesus spur you on to be His witness and to take the gospel to the ends of the earth?

❧ Write the final words you would like to give to others to encourage them to live wholeheartedly.

Resources to *restore*

Available in bookstores everywhere.

For information about these books or our authors visit NewHopeDigital.com. Experience sample chapters, podcasts, author interviews and more. Download the New Hope app for your iPad, iPhone, or Android!

Hold On
Finding Peace and Reward When God Has Us Waiting on Him
Debby Akerman
ISBN-13: 978-1-59669-390-6
N134131 $14.99

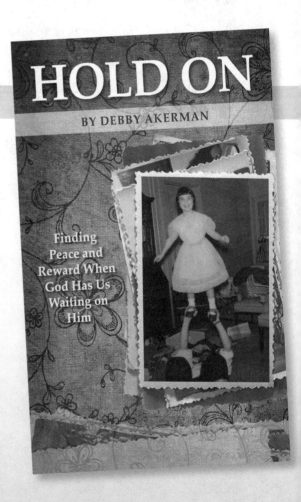

passion for God's call on your life!

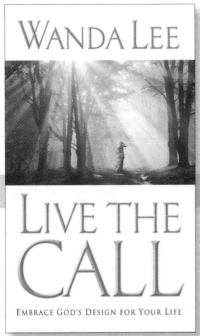

Live the Call
Embrace God's Design for Your Life
Wanda Lee
ISBN-13:
978-1-56309-994-6
N064127 $12.99

The Story Lives On
God's Power Throughout the Generations
Wanda S. Lee
ISBN-13:
978-1-59669-344-9
$14.99 N124149

New Hope® Publishers is a division of WMU®, an international organization that challenges Christian believers to understand and be radically involved in God's mission. For more information about WMU, go to wmu.com.
More information about New Hope books may be found at NewHopeDigital.com
New Hope books may be purchased at your local bookstore.

Use the QR reader on your
smartphone to visit us online at
NewHopeDigital.com

If you've been blessed by this book,
we would like to hear your story.
The publisher and author welcome your comments and
suggestions at: newhopereader@wmu.org.

WorldCrafts^{SM} develops sustainable, fair-trade businesses among impoverished people around the world. Each WorldCrafts product represents lives changed by the opportunity to earn an income with dignity and to hear the offer of everlasting life.

Visit WorldCrafts.org to learn more about WorldCrafts artisans, hosting WorldCrafts parties and to shop!

WORLDCRAFTS™

Committed. Holistic. Fair Trade.

WorldCrafts.org 1-800-968-7301

WorldCrafts is a division of WMU®

Engage.

Equip.

Encourage.

New Hope Publishers Women in Bible Study online community offers a place for women to engage with our best-selling Bible study authors, share experiences and insight, and learn of resources, both in print and online, that will help both Bible study leaders and participants grow deeper in their walk with Christ.

From relevant topics such as prayer, relationships, growth, lifestyle, and mentoring, there is something for women. Whether you've been engaged in Bible study your whole life or just getting started, the New Hope Women in Bible Study community will engage, equip, and encourage every woman seeking to live a godly life.

To learn more visit **NewHopeDigital.com/women**.

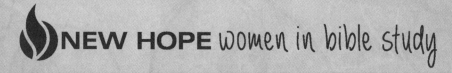